Network Security

Network Security

A practical guide

Owen Poole

LONDON AND NEW YORK

First published by Butterworth-Heinemann

First published 2003

This edition published 2012 by Routledge
2 Park Square, Milton Park, Abingdon, Oxon OX14 4RN
711 Third Avenue, New York, NY 10017, USA

Routledge is an imprint of the Taylor & Francis Group, an informa business

British Library Cataloguing in Publication Data
A catalogue record for this book is available from the British Library
ISBN: 978-0-7506-5033-5

Limit of liability

Contents

Contents

Contents

Computer Weekly Professional Series

There are few professions which require as much continuous updating as that of the IS executive. Not only does the hardware and software scene change relentlessly, but also ideas about the actual management of the IS function are being continuously modified, updated and changed. Thus keeping abreast of what is going on is really a major task.

Computer Weekly Professional Series has been created to assist IS executives keep up to date with the management ideas and issues of which they need to be aware.

One of the key objectives of the series is to reduce the time it takes for leading edge management ideas to move from the academic and consulting environments into the hands of the IT practitioner. Thus this series employs appropriate technology to speed up the publishing process. Where appropriate some books are supported by CD-ROM or by additional information or templates located on the Web.

This series provides IT professionals with an opportunity to build up a bookcase of easily accessible, but detailed information on the important issues that they need to be aware of to successfully perform their jobs.

Aspiring or already established authors are invited to get in touch with me directly if they would like to be published in this series.

Dr Dan Remenyi
Series Editor
dan.remenyi@mcil.co.uk

Preface

If you only do 10 things to make your network more secure, concentrate your effort in these areas:

1. Introduce best practice for passwords, ensuring passwords are never divulged to others.
2. Update and patch your operating system and application software.
3. Define and document your business continuity strategy.
4. Install and maintain up-to-date virus scanning software on servers and workstations.
5. Remove modems from desktop workstations and provide Internet access through one or more managed gateways.
6. Install a firewall that reflects your organization's approach to network security.
7. Prevent the use of VBScript and ActiveX content.
8. Introduce a policy for acceptable use of the World Wide Web and email.
9. Review the applicability of current legislation to your organization's activities.
10. Document your security policy.

Owen Poole

Acknowledgements

This book arose from a training course presented over the past few years to managers and executives from varied backgrounds. These people have greatly influenced the style and presentation of the ideas within this book. In addition, many of my colleagues have helped at various stages in the book's preparation. Special thanks go to Cy Marshall and Peter Newman, two people who played a significant part in the book's early stages. Finally, I would like to thank Catherine Werst for kindly allowing me to use her diagram as the basis for illustrating the OSI model in Chapter Two.

Security assessment

60% of organisations have suffered a security breach in the last two years.
(Information and Security Breaches Survey 2000,
UK Department of Trade and Industry)

Networked information systems, capable of storing, processing and delivering data on a global scale, are now part of many organizations' operational infrastructure. But, increased connectivity of information systems, in particular when using the Internet, brings about an unprecedented degree of risk. Computer viruses, for instance, can propagate throughout the connected world, via the Internet, in just a few hours. In the year 2000, circa 70 per cent of UK organizations were connected to the Internet[1] by some means, with circa 98 per cent of those larger organizations turning over in excess of £10 million per annum enjoying connectivity.[2] Yet, at the same time, concerns in the UK about network security were significant enough to be a barrier for greater exploitation of the Internet. In a recent KPMG survey,[2] 78 per cent of respondents said that the main obstacle to ecommerce was concern about security. These concerns are echoed in the results of similar surveys conducted in the USA.

Computer security is nothing new, though. Many organizations appear to have learnt lessons from the well-documented incidences of fraud that took place during the 1980s, and imposed various checks and measures on those who work with sensitive information. Personal background checks were advocated, software programming and maintenance activities were divided so that no single individual gained too much access and control by themselves, and organizations began to be aware that security was perhaps an issue that should be addressed. But, technology changes far faster than management practice, and if the continued reports in the media are a true indication of attitudes, then there is still a long way to go before the majority of organizations can claim to have fully addressed network security. Colloquial evidence, together with the repeated occurrence of similar types of security breaches, such as misuse of email, would suggest that many organizations are failing to tackle network security with the urgency required. The first step to turning this situation around is to accept that network security is an important issue worth addressing.

1.1 The importance of network security

Network security is an important issue, because of the dependence and utilization of computer networks in order to store, access, and provide business information, internally within an organization and externally to customers and suppliers. The information held on your organization's network plays a vital part in your organization's day-to-day operations. Everyone knows this, and if anyone has any doubt then take away their computer for a day or two! But, knowing this is often not enough to convince middle or senior management that network security is an important business issue.

In order to raise the profile of network security as a business issue, the value of information as a business asset and the cost of security breaches must first be appreciated. What is needed is some solid quantitative evidence. The good news is that there is plenty of evidence about.

The UK Department of Trade and Industry carry out a biannual information security survey among UK organizations. The latest survey[1] at the time of writing this book was carried out in 2000. Some of the key findings are summarized below, together with reference to a similar survey[2] conducted by the professional services firm KPMG. References to these reports discussed here and also some surveys published by other organizations[3-5] are listed at the end of the chapter.

1.1.1 Value of information held on networks

The majority of organizations surveyed, 69 per cent, hold information on their network that is classed as sensitive or critical.[1] The main reasons for the high value placed on the information were the perceived benefit to competitors, and the potential for loss of customer confidence in the event of disclosure.

1.1.2 Prevalence of security breaches

Between 1998 and 2000, 60 per cent of all organizations reported a security breach.[1] The main sources of reported breaches were user errors, viruses and power supply disruptions.

1.1.3 The financial cost of security breaches

Whatever the immediate consequences of network security breaches, though, the cost of the breaches will be measured ultimately in financial terms. In fact, the financial cost of security breaches makes a persuasive case to anyone who is sceptical of the importance of network security.

Those organizations that had a sufficiently enabled procedure for auditing breaches reported the cost of breaches to be anywhere **from £20 000 to in excess of £100 000 per breach**.[1] In all likelihood, the higher estimates are probably not too wide of the mark when the full impact of a security breach on the loss of productivity, loss of customer confidence, and adverse publicity are taken into account.

1.1.4 Security breaches are occurring more often

Most worryingly, given the apparent cost of security breaches, is that security breaches are on the increase according to KPMG. The increase is seen most notably in the areas of computer virus incidents, theft of computer equipment, and email intrusion.[2]

1.2 Network security is a business issue

The evidence reported within these surveys is compelling. The fact that the prevalence of security breaches is increasing, and the fact that each breach has the potential to cost so much money, means that network security is a business issue that requires management from the board level down throughout the entire organization. This is a salient point: the solution to network security does not rest with the IT department alone!

How long could you last?

Ask yourself this simple question: 'Without access to computerized information services such as invoicing, payroll, financial systems or email, how long could your organization continue to operate?' The answer may well be an extremely short period of time indeed. Some of the answers I have received to this question illustrate the point well. A global telecommunications company, which derives great competitive advantage in utilizing new technology, would grind to a halt within minutes if information on the main business systems, such as customer billing and invoicing, became unavailable. Another business, situated in the UK, that sells high-value specialized instrumentation found out the hard way that the logistics of managing meetings and conferences at their head office became unmanageable after just 20 minutes of their Microsoft Exchange Server being unavailable. For these organizations, the information stored on their network servers really is mission critical because they cannot operate when the information is unavailable.

But, organizations are not heeding this advice and network security continues to be perceived as an 'IT problem'. Computers and networks are installed by the IT department, so the IT department should take care of security as well, so the thinking goes. Indeed, KPMG[2] reported that 60 per cent of respondent organizations in their survey are laying responsibility for network security with their IT management teams. Laying responsibility with the IT department is perhaps one reason why, despite the strong advocacy of security policy by government, professional service firms, and other commentators, many organizations continue to tackle network security without any management framework or security policy.

A typical response by the IT department will be to install technical solutions such as firewalls, content controls, password controls, etc. All of these are valid responses to network security threats and many organizations base their response to network security threats around a varied mix of these technical solutions. There are, however, two key problems with this approach:

- Technical solutions can be readily installed, are more or less transparent to the user, and can continue to operate (ineffectively) with little ongoing maintenance. In other words, they are fit and forget solutions to network security. But, network security must never be seen in the context of fit and forget. The network security problem domain is ever changing, and the response must change accordingly. You must avoid the complacency that can be best illustrated by saying 'we have a firewall, we must be protected!' Of course, although they will continue to function without updating, technical solutions do require regular updating if they are to remain a truly effective means of protection. Otherwise their value will diminish rapidly.
- Technical solutions alone are only part of the overall solution. Technical solutions have a part to play in managing and monitoring users. They will do little, however, with regard to ensuring compliance with legal obligations, such as conformance to data protection legislation, for example. Generally speaking, technical solutions do not always take account of the people issues associated with secure use of computer networks.

Technical solutions are a key part of a security strategy, but they only constitute part of the response available to an organization and they often do little to influence workplace behaviour. Indeed, influencing workplace behaviour is not usually an area where the IT department are empowered to act. This guidance is often better off coming from other areas of the organization, such as the personnel department or, better still, the board of directors.

1.3 Management through security policy

One of the best ways of raising awareness and influencing behaviour is through a security policy. Yet, according to the DTI ISBS survey,[1] only 14 per cent of organizations in the UK have adopted a formal security policy. More than half of those questioned by the DTI, who had implemented a policy, reported their policy to be a good business practice, just over a fifth of those with a policy regard the policy as being a vital part of their legal compliance. Those who have implemented a policy have clearly found the policy to be a useful means of addressing security. This is further highlighted by the predominance of the financial and service industry sectors in having a security policy, either an in-house implementation of best practice or having based their policy on the BS 7799 accreditation. These organizations arguably stand to lose the most in the event of a network security breach! Statistics aside, there are other compelling reasons for using a policy to address network security:

- The policy defines the business requirement to protect information assets and services.
- Key risks arise from the people issues of educated use and acceptable use. One of the three main barriers to network security, identified by the NCC in their 2000 survey, was inadequate user awareness of security.
- The consequences of a security breach, financial or otherwise, will be felt throughout the organization.
- The needs of the entire organization can be met by tackling network security as an operational business issue, and developing a strategy to tackle identified risks.
- The security policy should also guide the deployment of technical solutions that act as a backup to the policy statements. Technical solutions are an essential part of the armoury that can protect an organization against security threats, but they need to be deployed in such a way that the operational practices and security requirements of the organization are reflected. This can only happen if deployment is driven by security policy. Installing technical solutions first, and writing policy second, is rather like putting the cart before the horse.

In addition, a well-constructed security policy serves several purposes that cannot be achieved by technical solutions alone:

- Education of users.
- A means of reprimanding users in the event of unacceptable or unauthorized use.
- The policy provides a proper management framework for addressing changes to threats and risks.

1.4 Defining the important issues

Network security embraces a diverse and broad range of concepts and issues. This diversity is one of the biggest barriers that managers face when attempting to get to grips with network security.

There are five key aspects to network security:

- First, there is the notion of *availability*, that the information and associated services provided by the secure network shall be available to intended users as and when required. This means, for instance, that product information on a website remains available to everyone at all times.
- Second, there is the notion of *integrity*, that information shall not be able to be subject to any unauthorized alteration, and shall not become corrupted for any reason. Users need to have confidence that the information they see is correct.
- Then there is the notion of *confidentiality*, that the information held on the secure network shall remain inaccessible to all those who have no need or privilege to see the information. For instance, sensitive business information shall be accessible to authorized parties only, and shall be protected against theft or espionage. Obviously the degree of confidentiality required depends on the nature of the information stored and on the nature of your organization. Government agencies or departments probably have different confidentiality requirements to some businesses.
- There is the protection of an organization's public reputation or legal standing through *acceptable use*, by ensuring that computers are used in an appropriate fashion.
- Finally, there is the definition and implementation of the appropriate *management framework* that aims to enhance and preserve security according to the four items specified above.

Bearing in mind the above criteria, a secure network can perhaps be defined in a nutshell as 'a network that is controlled by one or more appointed system administrators who grant access to information and services on a discretionary, controlled, and reviewed basis'.

In order to address network security systematically, the problem domain can be broken down into five main areas, which are addressed within this book:

1. Hardware and software configuration and maintenance.
2. Service configuration and access control.
3. Business continuity to help ensure availability.
4. User management to ensure legal and appropriate use of the computer network.
5. Technical solutions used to help ensure integrity and confidentiality.

Legacy hardware

One of the most commonly used storage devices, the floppy disk drive, is an Achilles' heel to many supposedly secure networks, enabling an easy and unauthorized source of access. Information can easily and discretely be copied to a floppy disk when a computer is inadvertently left unattended, whereupon all control of that information is lost. Moreover, most personal computers can be booted from a floppy disk regardless of what operating system may be stored on the hard drive, whereupon one of many security breaches could occur, unknown to the system administrator. Entire toolkits designed for this purpose can be made to fit upon just a couple of floppy disks. The hard drive can then be accessed, or the network traffic can be intercepted and captured. As computers become increasingly integrated by networks, in particular the Internet, there are few real uses for a floppy disk drive. But, computers continue to be fitted with this piece of redundant hardware as standard, and sales of floppy disks show no decline.

How it happens

Your organization employs a large number of staff, in a busy dynamic office. Deadlines are tight and the work is frantic. There is an important bid deadline, carried out with the utmost secrecy, looming at the end of the week and you have taken on a temporary assistant from a contract agency to help in the work. The temp arrives and you realize that you do not have a computer ready for him to use. Never mind, he can use the Internet terminal that is in the corner of the room. That machine has no password, meaning that anyone can use it. But, he will have to copy his work to a floppy disk and then take it onto your computer when he needs to use the printer.

The temp opens up a confidential document related to the bid and proceeds to start working. While still working on his document, other users pester him from time to time because they want to use the Internet computer. The temp replies that they can use the computer while he takes a coffee break.

In due course the temp saves his file and then goes on his

break. There is no need to close down his document because he wouldn't be long anyway. When he comes back he notices after a time that someone has taken his floppy disk from the computer. The disk had some other documents on it as well as that he was working on and a copy of the screensaver he had found on a website. He finds his floppy again, and then saves the document a second time and copies the saved file to floppy for printing out.

The temp wants to print out the work and asks to use your computer, but you're busy so you direct him to your colleague's computer as your colleague is on her tea break. The temp notices that the password-protected screensaver is in place and asks you for the password, so you tell him. The temp types the password into your colleague's computer and proceeds to use the word processing application to print out his work.

The next day, a virus is found on the office computer network. The file server is infected, so are computer networks in other offices. All computers connected to the network are shut down for three and a half hours, while the virus is identified and removed using anti-virus software updates. Work on the bid grinds to a halt during this time, after which there are further delays while fresh momentum is gathered by the team after the disruption.

1.5 The aims of the book

The primary aim of this book is to help you to implement protection for your organization against network security threats through policy and a proper management framework. Policy implementation does not require a deep technical knowledge, just an appreciation of the threats and of how to counteract those threats. To this end, technical issues are discussed wherever appropriate, but do be clear that this book does not contain a technical perspective on network security. There are plenty of other books available that do that and some are very good, so why reinvent the wheel? Many of those books, however, contain little discussion beyond the technical and there remains an 'implementation gap' of having read the technical perspective but still not having a clear way forward in your specific organization to addressing network security concerns.

Presumably, you are interested in making your organization's network secure and are interested in providing guidelines for acceptable use, through implementing a security policy of your own. This book will guide you through the various issues and problems that you will need to deal with, providing you with the necessary background information and practical knowledge to start tightening your organization's network security straight away. Action points are contained at the end of each chapter, leading toward the implementation of network security policy described in the final chapter of the book.

1.7 Review

- Network security is important because of the utilization and dependence on networked information systems.
- The majority of organizations surveyed have reported being hit by a breach of network security and, according to various reports, the incidence of breaches appears to be increasing.
- Network security is important to organizations because the financial cost of security breaches is large, in some cases in excess of £100 000 per breach.
- Security policy is the best way of managing an organization's response to network security threats, therefore reducing the incidence and cost of security breaches, educating users, and providing a means of exerting discipline in the event of misuse of the network.
- Network security encompasses availability, confidentiality and integrity of information, acceptable use of the network services, and the appropriate management framework.
- The five main areas of the security problem domain are hardware and software configuration and maintenance, service configuration and access control, disaster recovery, acceptable use, and implementation of technical measures.
- Various survey reports have been published which provide a broad discussion of information security, together with the attitudes and approaches of those organizations surveyed.

1.7 To do

1.7.1 Assessment of your organization's network security

A brief assessment of the importance of network security to organizations in general has been presented in this chapter. At this stage you are probably already thinking that you should be addressing network security in your organization. One of the first steps to addressing your network security is to carry out an initial assessment of your own operating environment. To start the ball rolling, here is a list of some of the questions you should be asking in the first instance. You may not know some of the answers at this stage. Never mind, there will be plenty of opportunity for you to pursue some of these lines of thought as you read through the remainder of this book. This is the first part in preparing for the implementation of a security policy:

- How secure is your network? (Circa one third of organizations rated their networks as average or less than average.[3])
- As a business asset, what value would you place upon the information stored on your network? (Sixty-nine per cent of organizations have information stored on their network classified as sensitive or critical.[1])
- How long could your organization continue to operate without use of the network? (Many organizations cannot operate for a few minutes without their network.)
- What would be the consequences of information being divulged to a third party?
- How do you control access to various parts of the computer network?
- Do users know how to choose appropriate passwords?
- Does your organization use the Internet? (Over 70 per cent of all organizations do, with nearly all large businesses being connected.[1,2])
- Do individuals have access to the World Wide Web from their desktop?
- Do you have a website? If so, is the website hosted by an ISP or by your own organization?
- What percentage of your revenue or marketing mix relies on ecommerce?
- What measures are in place to prevent users from installing their own software, for example from magazine cover discs?
- Do you have a business continuity plan?
- Have you or your IT department ever run auditing software on your network to assess weaknesses in the network?
- How long would your system administrators take to notice unauthorized access to your network?
- What formal procedures are there for reporting security breaches and assessing their impact?
- How many times have the following breaches occurred within your organization?
  1. Serious user error
  2. Power supply failure

3. Virus infection
4. Unauthorized access of data
5. Hardware or software failure
6. Theft of equipment
7. Unacceptable use, legal or otherwise

- Can you estimate the financial cost involved in any of these breaches?
- Who is responsible within your organization for your network security?
- Have you ever performed a formal risk assessment of your network security? (Just under 40 per cent of organizations have done so.[1])
- Does your organization have a network security policy? (As little as 14 per cent do![1])

1.8 References

1. Department of Trade and Industry (2000). *Information Security Breaches Survey 2000*. DTI. Also available are similar surveys from 1991, 1994, 1996 and 1998. These make interesting reading, and can be obtained from the DTI.
2. KPMG (2000). *Information Security Survey 2000*. KPMG. A report for 1998 is also available.
3. The National Computing Centre (2000). *The Business Information Security Survey (BISS 2000)*. NCC. Previous to this report, the NCC collaborated with the DTI in earlier surveys.
4. Computer Security Institute (2000). *2000 CSI/FBI Computer Crime and Security Survey*. CSI. This was the fifth report, each report published annually.
5. Ernst & Young (1999). *2nd Annual Global Information Security Survey*. Ernst & Young.

2

Network operating systems, protocols and services

The Internet ('Net) is a network of networks. Basically it is made from computers and cables.

(Tim Berners-Lee)

2.1 Network operating systems

Most computers require some sort of operating system to be installed if they are to do anything useful. The operating system performs various functions including:

- Manipulation of the computer processor and memory.
- Enabling data input and output, via the computer's peripherals such as the keyboard, mouse, modem, or network interface.
- Enabling other applications to be run on the computer, in order that the computer can be put to some meaningful use, by providing an interface between applications and the computer hardware in the form of an Application Program Interface, API for short.
- In many instances, providing support for multitasking, i.e. running more than one application concurrently.

In addition to the above criteria a network operating system also provides support for:

- Multiple users.
- Printer sharing.
- Shared data storage.
- Application hosting or shared data services.

The term 'network operating system' was used traditionally to define a set of programs that provided networking support to PCs that were using single user operating systems such as DOS. Using a network operating system enabled several of these PCs to be connected together in a local area network in order that resources could be shared locally throughout the workplace.

Examples of these early network operating systems include Banyan Vines, and Microsoft LAN Manager, but the most well-known example is Novell NetWare, which can be used with many other operating systems including DOS and Windows. Many of these early instances of network operating systems utilized proprietary means of communication, meaning that interoperability was sometimes an issue when attempting to connect different types of computers and operating systems together.

Although Novell NetWare remains a choice for some, demand for traditional network operating systems has declined considerably. This has been due to the widespread adoption of TCP/IP, the open means of communications used on the Internet, together with the widespread adoption of desktop computers networked with Microsoft Windows. Contemporary operating systems, such as Windows and Unix, perform many of the networking functions of the early add-on network operating systems as standard.

2.2 Security features

Central to the network operating systems are the various features that facilitate security. The way in which these various features are combined within any particular operating system is termed the operating system's security model. A security model will contain some or all of the following features.

2.2.1 User authentication

A network operating system has access controls for the various user accounts, usually using account names and passwords. To use an account, each user will need to provide a valid user name and associated password in order to log on. This process of providing a password is sometimes referred to as authentication. By the provision of a correct account password, the user is confirming that they really do have access to the particular account they are attempting to log on to.

The computer has no way of distinguishing between a user who is authorized to use an account, and an unauthorized user who has obtained or guessed the account password. Clearly, for password authentication to work, account passwords must not be divulged, otherwise their value will be lost.

Because of the risks associated with passwords being divulged or otherwise being found out by a third party, other means of user authentication are used in some instances. There are biometric authentication methods available such as finger-print scanners, or methods that require swipe or smart cards to be used.

2.2.2 Object access control

An object within a computer can be thought of as files, such as data files or application files, folders and directories, or resources attached to the computer, such as printers. Access to objects can be controlled by setting object access rights for single user accounts or by groups of users. The access control's attributes are sometimes referred to as permissions. For instance, a file can be set so that only certain user accounts are able to change the file contents, but every account can read the file contents. Accounts that create or own objects often have the authority to change access controls if desired so that the account user can heighten or lessen the level of security.

2.2.3 User groups

Each user account belongs to one or more user groups and each group has access permissions to various parts of the computer file system. Most accounts belong to a general 'user' group, but a limited number of accounts belong to an 'administrator' group. The administrator group, as the name suggests, carries rather more privilege than the user group, and members of that group are able to exercise absolute control over the computer operating system. As a consequence, system administrators can wield an enormous amount of power over a system. In addition to the administrator groups, there are other groups that have varying degrees of access and rights, typically these groups may have permission to make backups or conduct other limited administrative duties.

2.2.4 Application privilege

Given that an account has access to files and resources controlled by the appropriate application of permissions, any application that is executed by the user account should inherit the same permissions as the account itself. This means that a word processor should inherit the permissions of the account using the application, and should not be able to open documents that do not have file permissions granting at least read access by that user account. Otherwise, a user could open up documents they should not be able to view, or worse still change them.

2.2.5 Encryption

Often, controlling user access by the use of authenticated accounts and setting appropriate access controls is enough to ensure that data is safeguarded. In some situations, such as in a networked environment where a large part of the network is public, i.e. the Internet, data may be travelling over large distances, where the route travelled by the data, and therefore access to the data, cannot be controlled. In such instances, other means of safeguarding data are sought. One means of safeguarding data is to make the data appear unintelligible except to those who you wish to read the data.

Encryption is a means of making data appear unintelligible to unauthorized third parties. Data that has been encrypted cannot usually be read without the appropriate key to decrypt the data. Possession of the key is restricted to certain parties. Data can be encrypted on a hard drive or can be encrypted prior to transmission over an insecure network such as the Internet.

2.2.6 Distributed authentication

At the time when large LANs were being set up, the need arose for users within large campus networks to be able to access their accounts on any computer within that network. The means to provide user authentication over a network rather than at a single computer was therefore developed. The implementation, Kerberos, has been observed to be particularly secure and, as such, Kerberos is now a widely used means of distributed authentication.

2.2.7 Accessibility

The accessibility of the inner workings of an operating system is perhaps less important to some than other security features. Nevertheless, the extent to which an administrator or security specialist can examine the inner workings of the operating system arguably contributes to the overall system security. Some operating systems are so accessible that the programming source code is available on the Internet for anyone to download, examine, change and recompile.

The argument for accessibility being a contributory factor to security is that the more accessible an operating system is to the public domain, the more likely that bugs are discovered and then subsequently corrected. If the inner workings of an operating system are closely guarded, then bugs may be present, but may not be addressed until enough people are aware of their existence. Another advantage of wider accessibility is a greater ability to tailor an operating system to specific hardware, for resilience or speed advantages, or more ability to configure the operating system. Greater accessibility, though, does not always imply easier configuration.

2.3 Client/Server networking

The concept of client/server networking is central to virtually all computer networks in operation today. The client/server architecture gained in popularity during the late 1980s, arising out of the need to connect desktop personal computers together in order to share office resources, such as printers and disk space, in a local area network. Now, the Internet provides the infrastructure for various client/server applications, and a Web client such as Internet Explorer, for example, can be used to browse pages from a Web server somewhere else on the Internet.

2.3.1 The server

A server is a software application that provides network resources and services on request by a network client. The server application is active only when the services are being delivered to a requesting client. When services are not being requested the server application is idle, waiting and listening for incoming requests. Examples of commonly used server applications include Web servers, email servers, database servers, etc. In the context of Unix operating systems, server applications are sometimes referred to as daemons.

2.3.2 The client

The client is the software application that requests network services. Perhaps the most well-known client software application is the Web browser, other examples include email clients, database interfaces, etc. As is the case of Web browsers, client applications are often used to provide an interface for the information requested by end users.

In order for the client/server architecture to work, though, there needs to be an efficient means of communicating information, from client to server and back again, across a network. This is the job of the underlying network protocol.

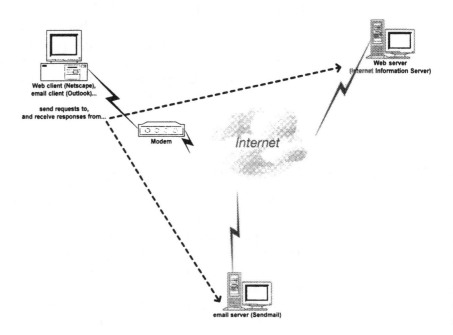

Figure 2.1
The client/server model on the Internet

2.4 Network protocol

For the client/server model to work, the client and server applications must be able to communicate and share data. Within computer networks, a protocol is a set of rules governing data exchange. As an analogy, a protocol can be thought of as a common language by which two software applications can communicate with each other. There are various types of protocol, but they can all be placed in one of two categories, proprietary protocols or open protocols. We shall be concentrating our attention on open protocols, in particular on the TCP/IP protocol suite used on the Internet and also on most private corporate networks.

2.5 TCP/IP

The TCP/IP protocol suite is a collection of protocols that were developed during the operation of the DARPAnet, the Internet forerunner. With the growth of the Internet, TCP/IP has become the de-facto standard for corporate networking. The TCP/IP protocol suite has been implemented in all operating systems in common use today, and is used as standard within the Unix and Microsoft Windows operating systems.

TCP/IP stands for Transmission Control Protocol and Internet Protocol. As this implies, TCP/IP is in fact two separate but closely tied protocols, each one performing a distinct purpose.

- The TCP part of TCP/IP is responsible for breaking up data or information originating from a network service into small pieces, which are often called packets, suitable for transmission over the network. TCP is connection oriented in that a connection is required before data can be transmitted. Also, error checking is carried out within TCP and so there is usually no loss during transmission when using TCP. Data is received in the correct order required for reassembly.
- The IP part of TCP/IP is responsible for the actual addressing and transmission of packets across the network. There is no guarantee of successful transmission and receipt with IP, that is the role of TCP within TCP/IP.

There are, however, other protocols used besides TCP and IP. The most common of these is a protocol called UDP, User Datagram Protocol. Whereas TCP requires a connection, UDP does not need a connection before sending data. Thus, data is streamed across a network with no attention paid to whether the information was received or not.

ICMP is another protocol, and is used by the ping utility in order to check the function of a network. ICMP also enables two parts of a network to share status and error information. ICMP is short for Internet Control Message Protocol.

2.6 Network addressing

In order to send data back and forth across a network, we need to assign network addresses. Unless there is to be confusion, these need to be unique within each physical network. As an analogy, just as each telephone in the world has a unique telephone number, so each computer on a network must have a unique IP address, and that includes every computer connected to the Internet!

Network addresses are assigned to network interfaces such as network interface cards or modems. Hardware such as computers can be assigned more than one network address by virtue of having more than one interface installed.

2.6.1 MAC address

The MAC address is the fundamental address of each network interface device, and is embedded into the device during manufacture. MAC is short for Media Access Control, and each MAC address is unique. When connected to the network a lookup table is used to reference the computer's IP address to the computer's MAC address. The MAC address is usually represented in hexadecimal format, e.g. the address of the 3COM Ethernet card in my PC at the moment is 00-A0-24-99-47-73. The first half is unique to each manufacturer, and the second half is unique to the interface.

2.6.2 IP addresses

Each IP address is in the form of a 32-bit binary number, which is usually converted into dotted decimal format, with four parts, this format being more user friendly. Each part of the IP address can range from 0 to 255.

An example address is 192.168.1.10, which in this case is the IP address of my PC. This particular address is part of a range of addresses reserved for closed networks, 192.168.0.0 to 192.168.255.255. These particular addresses are reserved for private use and data cannot travel from one private network directly to another. Use of private addressing therefore avoids potential conflict when private networks use the Internet. Another notable IP address is the address 127.0.0.1, which is the default IP address of every computer, and again is a reserved address. There are various addressing schemes, but these are beyond the scope of this book.

2.6.3 Subnet mask

The subnet mask is used to distinguish network addresses from host addresses in a network. The subnet mask also defines a range of host IP addresses. For instance:

- The range 192.168.1.0 to 192.168.1.255 would have a subnet mask 255.255.255.0.
- The range 192.168.0.0 to 192.168.255.255 would have a subnet mask 255.255.0.0.

The 0 in the subnet mask represents the host parts of the network address range that will change within a network addressing scheme, the 255 represents the fixed parts of the network address.

Alternatively, the subnet mask can be represented in each case as 192.168.1.0/24 or 192.168.0.0/16. This is because in each case, if the numbers were written in binary format, the first 24 or 16 bits (i.e. the first 3, or first 2 dotted decimals) respectively would remain fixed throughout the address range specified.

2.6.4 Network address

The subnet mask is used in conjunction with each device's IP address to define which particular computer network the interface device belongs to. This network address is derived by placing a zero within the IP address location corresponding to each 0 in the subnet mask.

- The network address for 192.168.1.34 with subnet mask 255.255.255.0 is 192.168.1.0.
- The network address for 192.168.34.35 with subnet mask 255.255.0.0 is 192.168.0.0.

2.6.5 Gateway address

A gateway is required if communication is to be made to other devices on another network, the Internet, for example. The gateway address is usually similar to the network address, having a one at the end of the address instead of a zero. All TCP/IP messages meant for destinations that lie outside the immediate network, i.e. to other networks, are directed to the gateway. Typically, there might be a router situated at the gateway.

- The gateway address for 192.168.1.0 would usually be 192.168.1.1.

2.7 IP ports

The TCP/IP protocol suite uses numbered ports to facilitate connections between servers and clients. By convention, each particular service on a computer uses a defined fixed port number to listen out for requests. Thus, when sending the outgoing request, the client application is able to specify the server application required in response. A Web server, for instance, generally uses port 80 by default to listen for incoming requests. So, all requests made by a Web browser – the client – to a particular IP address are made to the destination port 80.

You should be careful to distinguish between a transmission port and a destination port. Outgoing network messages originate from dynamically allocated ports, and the port used for outgoing data transmissions will vary according to availability, regardless of the service being used. Only the destination port is fixed. This is of particular importance when trying to control the flow of network traffic, with a firewall for instance, using port numbers as criteria by which traffic should pass through or be halted.

Port numbers range from zero to 65 536, with ports zero to 1024 reserved for use by specific services. Ports above 1024 are free for use, and are used as dynamically allocated transmission ports by computers in a network. Some of these ports are nevertheless sometimes used by specific services. A list of port numbers used by some more commonly used services is contained within Table 2.1. The table contains the briefest of summaries relating to port numbers allocated to various services. More information can be found in the IANA list on the Web, the URL is:

http://www.isi.edu/in-notes/iana/assignments/port-numbers

Table 2.1 Port numbers

Port	Protocol	Service	Comment
13	TCP, UDP	daytime	Daytime
17	TCP, UDP	qotd	Quote of the day
20	TCP	ftp-data	File Transfer
21	TCP	ftp	FTP Control
22	TCP	SSh	Secure Shell
23	TCP	telnet	Telnet
25	TCP	smtp	Simple Mail Transfer
37	TCP, UDP	time	Time
42	TCP, UDP	nameserver	Host Name Server
43	TCP	nicname	Who Is
53	TCP, UDP	domain	Domain Name
69	UDP	tftp	Trivial File Transfer
70	TCP	gopher	Gopher
79	TCP	finger	Finger
80	TCP	http	World Wide Web
88	TCP, UDP	kerberos	Kerberos
107	TCP	rsh	Remote Telnet Service
110	TCP	pop3	Post Office Protocol V3
119	TCP	nntp	Network News Transfer Protocol
137	TCP, UDP	netbios-ns	SMB: nbname NETBIOS Name Service
138	UDP	netbios-dgm	SMB: nbdatagram NETBIOS Datagram Service
139	TCP	netbios-ssn	SMB: nbsession NETBIOS Session Service
143	TCP	imap	imap4 Internet Message Access Protocol
161	UDP	snmp	SNMP
162	UDP	snmptrap	SNMP TRAP
194	TCP	irc	Internet Relay Chat Protocol
213	UDP	ipx	IPX over IP
389	TCP	ldap	Lightweight Directory Access Protocol
443	TCP, UDP	https	Secure http
464	TCP, UDP	kpasswd	Kerberos (v5)
500	UDP	isakmp	Internet Key Exchange (IPSec)
512	UDP	biff	Comstat, notifies users of new mail
517	UDP	talk	Establishes TCP Connection
531	TCP	conference	IRC Chat
543	TCP	klogin	Kerberos login
544	TCP	kshell	krcmd, Kerberos remote shell
636	TCP	ldaps	sldap, LDAP over TLS/SSL
666	TCP, UDP	Doom	Popular game
749	TCP, UDP	krbrs-adm	Kerberos administration
>1024		NetMeeting	Web conferencing
1352	TCP	Lotus Notes	Lotus Notes Domino
1863	TCP	MSN Messenger	Messaging service
5190	TCP, UDP	Instant Messenger	Messaging service
5190	TCP	AOL ICQ	Messaging service
5190–3	TCP, UDP	AOL	America On Line
7070	TCP	Real	Real Audio and Video
6970–7170	UDP	Real	Real Audio and Video
14 237	TCP	Hotsync	Palm computing network
14 238	UDP	Hotsync	Palm computing network
26 000	TCP, UDP	Quake	Popular game

2.8 The domain name system

Of course, when using a network such as the Internet, there is no need for anyone to remember IP addresses. Instead, computers on the Internet are identified by the use of domain names. The domain name system, DNS, is a means of relating IP addresses to domain names. The thinking behind DNS is that people can remember www.yahoo.com more easily than the corresponding IP address of the yahoo Web server.

Domain names are relatively straightforward to understand, the main feature being that there are two types of domain name, the generic domain names of the .com variety, and then the country specific domain name, for example .co.uk. This situation has arisen by virtue of the generic top-level domain names being defined at such a time when the Internet was largely based in the US, so that country of origin was not an issue. The various generic top-level domain names are listed in Table 2.2 together with their meaning. Domain names using these top-level names are allocated on a first come first served basis, by domain name registries, in the case of the US, by the InterNIC.

Table 2.2 Generic top-level domain names

.com	Commercial organization
.edu	US academic organization
.gov	US government
.mil	US military
.net	Internet infrastructure, such as service providers
.org	Non-profit making organization

As the Internet grew in extent, countries preferred to define their own domain name schemes and to set up their associated registries. In the UK, the second level indicates the activity. Various UK second-level domain names are listed in Table 2.3. Third-level derivatives are again available on a first come first served basis; in the UK, these domain names are awarded by Nominet. The format used by other countries varies. Some countries, such as France or Germany, omit the second-level activity identifier, and simply have the unique identifier followed by the country identifier; compare for example www.yahoo.fr or www.yahoo.de to www.yahoo.co.uk.

Table 2.3 UK Domain Names

.ac.uk	UK academic organizations
.co.uk	UK commercial organization
.gov.uk	UK government
.mod.uk	UK Ministry of Defence
.net.uk	Internet infrastructure, such as service providers
.nhs.uk	The National Health Service
.org.uk	Organization that does not fit in any of the other classifications
.police.uk	The police
.sch.uk	UK schools

2.8.1 DNS server

When a Web client is used, and the domain name www.yahoo.com is typed into the address window, there has to be a way of referring the domain name to the correct IP address used by the yahoo website server. There are two ways this can be achieved.

The first way would be to maintain a list of all the known domain names against all their known IP addresses. To be effective, this list would need to be comprehensive and be updated at regular intervals.

The second way would be to let someone else maintain such a list, and then have your computer query that list whenever you wish to access a computer at a particular domain name. This is what most people do. Usually, lists of IP addresses and domain names are maintained by Internet service providers, or sometimes by large organizations that have a permanent connection to the Internet, universities, for example. This list is made available to others on a DNS server, sometimes called a nameserver. The DNS server to be used is identified by a specified IP address, obviously one could not refer to a DNS server by domain name! Usually the DNS IP address is provided by your system administrator, and is included within the networking configuration files or network properties of your operating system.

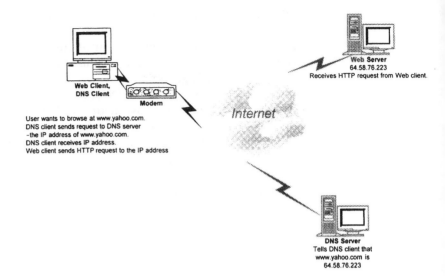

Figure 2.2

2.9 The paradox of using TCP/IP

TCP/IP is not the most secure means for network communications on a private or secure network. Although TCP provides some degree of resilience by accurate packet reassembly and error checking, IP provides no such checks and safeguards. In fact the IP protocol does not even have the facility to guarantee the origin of data, as represented by the IP address in the packet header. This IP address can be easily faked, or spoofed, so as to mask the true origin of the transmission. Rather more disturbing is the fact that TCP/IP network transmissions within a network can be eavesdropped by any other interface on the network, using the appropriate software such as a network analyser. In other words, anyone on the same local network as you can easily capture and read the data you are sending or receiving – email, for instance, or credit card numbers.

There within lies the paradox. TCP/IP is an open network protocol. Specifications for the protocol are freely available, as are client software applications. This means that when you use TCP/IP on a network, you are opening up your computer to potentially every other computer on that network. But, this protocol is being used for private and secure networking. How private and secure can that be?

2.10 Common TCP/IP services

2.10.1 Telnet

The telnet client and server applications provide a means to access and use a remote host computer from a command line interface. Using a telnet client, a user can issue commands at the prompt as if he or she were sitting at the remote host directly. Telnet can, and often is, used to issue commands remotely across the Internet.

Telnet is a service usually associated with Unix, in which there are telnet clients and servers installed often by default. But, telnet can also be used within Windows, where a telnet client is provided, with the option to install or activate the telnet server if desired so that shell commands can be issued remotely.

Using telnet is straightforward. All the user requires is access to an account on the remote computer, together with a telnet client. Of course, the remote computer must also be running a telnet server. The telnet client is usually started by the command 'telnet' followed by the IP address or the domain name of the remote computer, from within a command shell. A telnet connection is then initiated, and the server presents a login prompt to the client, for the user to present an account name and password.

The telnet client essentially performs two functions first, the transmission of the user's keyboard input to the remote server, and then the display of the remote server's output. The server then presents a command line interface to the client display, executing commands on the remote computer as if the user were interfacing with the computer directly.

2.10.2 FTP

FTP is an abbreviation for File Transfer Protocol, and as the name suggests, an FTP client and server enables users to transfer files from one host to another, which may be some physical distance away. FTP was used a great deal before the advent of the World Wide Web for the distribution of software patches and fixes and also as a means of enabling documentation to be distributed among the academic community, and latterly the business community. These days FTP has in many instances been superseded by the Web, most people only use FTP to upload html documents to remote Web servers. There are still FTP sites available, though, and in some ways FTP is a superior means of transmitting information, providing faster download rates and better resilience.

FTP clients and servers are usually installed by default with Unix operating systems. Microsoft Windows server editions have the option to install an FTP server, part of IIS, during the installation routine, and an FTP client is installed by default as part of the TCP/IP networking suite. The functionality of FTP on these operating systems is very similar, resembling superficially a telnet session. Some, however, find the command line prompt of basic FTP clients awkward to use, and there have been a great many GUI FTP clients written that provide the means to transfer files by the familiar drag and drop interaction similar to using the Windows Explorer.

The basic plain vanilla client is usually executed from the command line by the command FTP followed by the IP address of domain name of the remote computer. A prompt for an account name and password is made, after which the user may then execute the appropriate commands to transfer files.

There are two types of account that may be used, login can be made via a normal user account, or by using the anonymous login facility designed to make files accessible to the general network community.

2.10.3 NNTP

NNTP stands for Network News Transfer Protocol and is the protocol that enables Usenet news to be sent and delivered between remote computers. Usenet news is a 'bulletin board'-like way of exchanging short messages and attachments within a group of like-minded users. Usenet news is perhaps not as well-known in the UK as in the United States and in other countries, largely because the World Wide Web superseded news groups to a large degree.

The Usenet network enables articles to be posted on large bulletin boards that are updated and replicated the world over. News items are split into groups and there are in excess of 50 000 news groups that embrace almost any subject that you could imagine. By reading a news group, users can then download individual articles of news and then perhaps post their own articles continuing the discussion. Newsgroups can be accessed without using NNTP, there are several websites that archive and allow posting to groups. One such site is groups.google.com.

2.10.4 SMTP

SMTP is an abbreviation for Simple Mail Transfer Protocol, and is the de-facto standard for sending and receiving email across the Internet, and has therefore become a standard for messaging on smaller closed networks, such as office LANs. The SMTP server is found mainly on computers running Unix, although Microsoft Exchange can also run an implementation of SMTP called Internet Service. The most well-known email server is Sendmail, a complex application for which there have been a number of very large books written.

2.10.5 HTTP

Short for HyperText Transfer Protocol, HTTP is the protocol that enables documents to be distributed on the World Wide Web. Arguably, use of HTTP clients and servers on the Internet was the main reason for the extremely rapid growth the Internet experienced in the 1990s.

2.10.6 SMB

SMB stands for Server Message Block, and is the protocol used by Microsoft to deploy network services such as files, printers, and serial ports, from servers to various clients, within many operating systems, including in the past Windows for Workgroups, Windows 95, and more recently Windows NT 4 and Windows 2000. The SMB client connects to the SMB server, which then provides the browser service that enables client workstations to browse and access the resources provided by the server.

SMB is essentially a Microsoft Windows-oriented service, but there are client and server implementations of SMB available for other platforms, including Digital Pathworks, LAN Manager for OS/2, SCO Unix and others, which help integrate heterogeneous computers or provide enhanced services. Indeed, SMB has been gaining popularity within the Unix community lately, by virtue of the freely available server application, Samba, released for Linux and other Unix distributions, which provides equivalent services to a Windows server.

2.10.7 LDAP

LDAP is short for Lightweight Directory Access Protocol (lightweight because the implementation is a reduced version of the Directory Access Protocol that is part of the X.500 standard). The protocol is used to enable resources such as files and printers to be located on a network. Developed by the University of Michigan, LDAP has now been used by many vendors such as

Netscape, and also Microsoft in the Active Directory structure. Cisco also supports LDAP within various hardware products.

Usually, in order to use resources on a network you need to know the IP address or domain name of where those resources are located. LDAP, however, works by enabling searches for network resources to be made without knowing where they are located. The LDAP directory is organized in a hierarchical structure, starting from a root and then extending to Countries, Organizations, Departments, and then to individual entries such as files, printers, and people. With the release of Windows 2000 and the Active Directory, LDAP services are being increasingly widely used.

2.11 The seven layer model

This section can be skipped if you have had enough of networking, although you might want to jump back here when you read the firewall chapter. If you can read through this and follow the points, then congratulations are due as this is as technical as the book gets!

The OSI reference model is a conceptual model composed of seven layers, each specifying particular network functions. The model is a standard description of how data communication can be implemented between two points on a network, and was adopted as a standard by the ISO and is also recommendation X.200 of the ITU-TS.

Each layer contains specific functionality and requires the presence of the lower levels before communication can take place. This means that in a communication between two computers, data is sent down the layers on the transmission computer, transmitted to the destination computer whereupon the data is sent back up through the layers and then used for whatever the intended purpose was. Each layer can interact with the layers above, or below, or with the equivalent layer on the destination address (Figure 2.3).

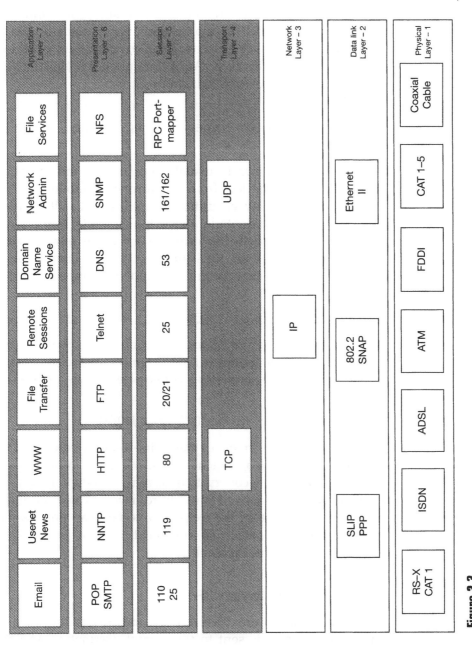

Figure 2.3
Open Systems Interconnection OSI seven layer model

The seven layers are described briefly below:

7 – Application layer (email, web applications, Usenet news, File transfer, etc.)

The application layer is where the network communication interfaces with the software application that is communicating data over a network. The application layer is used to send or receive data, and issues such as service use and authentication are taken care of at this layer. As a consequence of this functionality, this layer is closest to the end user.

6 – Presentation layer (smtp, http, nntp, ftp, etc.)

The presentation layer is usually the part of the operation system that converts data from one format to another, so that information sent between different applications will be readable. Instances of presentation-layer functionality include data representation in specific file formats, such as the representation of image files in GIF or JPEG formats. The presentation layer will also deal with data compression and encryption schemes.

5 – Session layer (25, 80, 119, 21, etc.)

The session layer co-ordinates and manages communication sessions between presentation layer instances, including requests for services and responses that occur between clients and servers.

4 – Transport layer (TCP, UDP)

The transport layer manages the point-to-point control of the network transmission, functions include flow control, error checking, and error recovery, to determine whether all data has arrived. One of the jobs of flow control is to ensure that data is not received faster that the recipient interface can process. The most common example of transport control is TCP, the Transmission Control Protocol.

3 – Network layer (IP)

The network layer provides routing and forwarding of data, ensuring that data is sent to the correct destination and that data is received appropriately. The network layer supports both connection protocols and connectionless protocols.

Network-layer protocols are usually routing protocols, such as IP, the Internet Protocol; other instances include OSPF, the Open Shortest Path First, and RIP, the Routing Information Protocol.

2 – Data link layer (Ethernet)

The data link layer ensures successful transmission of data across the physical network. Specifications within this layer include synchronization of data and flow control.

1 – Physical layer (coaxial cables)

The physical layer deals with the actual transmission of the electrical signal through the communication medium, and might include specification for voltage, transmission rates, etc. This layer deals with the wires, cables, interface cards, and other networking hardware.

2.12 Review

- A network operating system performs various functions such as print and file sharing, data storage, application hosting, and centralized data services, and includes common network protocols for communication with other computers.
- Network operating systems generally include user authentication, object access control, user groups, application privilege, and sometimes include support for encryption and remote authentication; collectively these features are termed the security model.
- A server is a software application that provides information to a client software application at the request of the client, for example Web pages stored on a server are sent to a client Web browser following a request made by the user.
- A protocol is a set of rules governing data exchange so that data communication can take place between two computers on a network.
- Data communications is often discussed with reference to the seven layer model.
- The MAC address is an address hardwired within a network interface card or similar device.
- The IP address is the unique address given to a computer on a TCP/IP network, for instance the Internet; however, some IP addresses are reserved for use on private networks.
- TCP/IP data transmission can be characterized by the

transmission and destination IP addresses and the transmission ports and destination listening ports.
- The domain name system is used to map domain names onto IP addresses.
- TCP is an inherently insecure means of transmitting data.
- Common protocols which use TCP/IP include telnet, FTP, NNTP, SMTP, HTTP, SMB and LDAP.
- Each protocol is characterized by a default listening port number.

2.13 To do

If your organization is in a similar position to most, you will most likely find that there are several operating systems within your organization's information network. In other words you have a heterogeneous network. This state of affairs may have arisen, due to procuring computers at different times or from different vendors, or to the need to continue to support legacy applications. This is not as crass as it might sound. Even in 2001, I visited a blue chip business that was only just upgrading from Windows 3.1!

- You should consider planning a strategy for having a single O/S on the majority of desktops, and if possible a single operating system on the server. Also you should think carefully about what operating system you want to be running your Internet facing applications.
- The choice of operating system should be dictated by various criteria, such as ease of use and support, application availability, resilience, and stability. As far as the desktop is concerned the vast majority of organizations choose some version of Microsoft Windows. An outside contender might be Apple OSX or similar. These operating systems are easy to use and support a range of productivity applications.
- For server applications, there is a wider choice, with Unix being a serious contender alongside Microsoft Windows and also Novell NetWare.
- Above all, you should be sure that your policy for operating system installation is based on a proper examination of operational requirements and is not created ad hoc by whatever operating system is supplied with the computers that you procure.

2.13.1 Familiarize yourself with some networking utilities

Go to your computer, perhaps in a test lab you have set-up, and let's see what we can do with a command prompt!

Windows users

Windows users can carry out a fair amount of investigation when logged on as a normal user by the use of the command prompt shell, although administrative users will be able to use the Network Properties Window to see more detailed information.

* Open up the command shell.
* Now type the command *ipconfig/all.*
* Note the information returned includes your IP address, gateway address, subnet mask, and the description and MAC address of the interface used.
* You can view the same information by clicking on the appropriate network icon and selecting the properties tab. The exact location of the window varies within different editions of Windows, but Network Neighborhood or My Network Places is a good place to look.

Unix users

Unix users can obtain the same information:

* Open up a command prompt.
* Type the command *ifconfig.*
* Note the information returned includes your IP address, gateway address, subnet mask, and the description and MAC address of the interface used.

More information

* Now for some text commands. Open up a command prompt or command shell.
* First, try to ping yourself, using the command *ping 127.0.0.1.*
* That should work, so now try ping <your IP address>. If you are unsure of your address, try the commands given above.
* Next, try to ping your default gateway.
* OK, now type netstat. The return gives a list of all the open network connections. This command can be used with switches or options so that the return updates every *n* seconds.

- Got a Unix computer handy with an account? Perhaps your ISP provides you with a Unix logon. Try and use the telnet command to connect to your account. If you can get connected, then type netstat again. Can you spot your connection?

- Now, let's use telnet to access some specific ports. *Try telnet <Domain Name of your Web server> 80*. You are now accessing the Web server of your company, with the response being sent back to your command prompt. Usually, unless you can type http commands at the prompt, you will kill the connection as soon as you type anything. If you have an http reference manual, you may be able to work out the command used to get a Web page.

- Try to telnet to the smtp port, i.e. port 25. You might get a return which specifies exactly what email server you are using! When I did this to my Linux computer, I got a response stating '220 pukka.poole.lan ESMTP Sendmail 8.9.3/8.9.3; Tue, 1 May 2001 13:40:02 GMT'. If you get a similar response, try the command *help*. You can see that if you are a real techie, you could start to find out a great deal about a server just using telnet alone!

3   The threats to a secure network

Better a thousand enemies outside your house than one within.

(Arabic proverb)

3.1 Introduction

Often, when people discuss network security, conversation quickly turns to computer cracking by people who gain unauthorized access into computer systems. The film *War Games* is often recalled, where Matthew Broderick manages to break into a Pentagon computer with just a very basic PC in his bedroom! But, as any of the surveys of the main causes of security breaches show, significant as instances of cracking are, they are not the only instances of security breaches. Nor are they by any stretch of the imagination the most prevalent or widespread. The actual situation is rather more mundane, but also rather more manageable.

The most common cause of security breach according to the DTI ISBS 2000 survey was user error. Power supply faults and virus infection also figured prominently. These findings underline, in a very empirical way, the folly of basing security policy solely on technical solutions such as firewalls. Spending money on technical solutions alone diverts your budget from the number one cause for security breaches, the users themselves. Diverting some budget towards user training might prevent many more breaches that occur due to user error and other human interventions, than investing in technical solutions alone.

The key to targeting the threats to the secure network in your organization is first to establish threat awareness, and then to determine the likelihood of each of the main threats occurring. So, let's review each of the main threats in turn.

3.2 Users: the threat from within!

To many who are just starting to look into security, one of the most surprising points is that the main threat comes not from the cracker on the Internet, although this threat should not be underestimated, but from those who use the computer network on a daily basis. That is to say, that most security breaches occur from within an organization as a result of the actions of the organization's own staff. Many estimates put the figure of user derived security breaches at as much at 60 per cent, by far the most common source of security breach.

This is not to presume that security breaches due to users arise out of any malicious action. Security breaches are often caused by ignorance or by human error. Many users are somewhat ignorant about the consequences of their actions and the impact their actions have on security. Also many system administrators underestimate the amount of user education and training users require on an ongoing basis, not just on how to use respective applications, but also on general IT orientation and awareness of acceptable and appropriate use.

Case Study – User error

Here are some various incidences, all of them true, in which users actions can cause security breaches with absolutely no malicious action or intent on their part whatsoever!

- A user plays around with their computer settings, changes the IP address for the network adapter, and causes IP address duplication, forcing either themselves or someone else to be unable to access the network. This is not possible using Windows NT, 2000, etc., but is possible using Windows 98 or ME, versions of Windows in use by many organizations.
- A copy of network *Doom* is discovered on a cover disk dating back a few years, is brought into the workplace, and installed on a few of the desktop PCs for use at lunchtime. Of course the game playing gains popularity. On early versions, network broadcast messages are sent which can flood the network capacity. As more people join in the multiplayer game the

network grinds to a halt. This situation occurred in many offices, and caused so many problems to the extent that playing *Doom* was a dismissable offence in some organizations.

- A senior manager who uses the Internet frequently to browse the World Wide Web bypasses the secure connection through the LAN gateway by installing and using a modem. This is because the modem offers a more responsive connection. The modem creates a backdoor from the Internet into the network, and as a consequence the network is no longer secure. Data is able to flow through the modem without any of the content control or access controls that the secure gateway provides.
- A user decides to explore the Windows registry and change a few settings to 'optimize' his computer. When the computer is rebooted, the system is inoperable. This is only possible if the administrator password is known, but many users have the administrative password for their own local administrative account.
- A programmer reads about the 'Back Orifice' utility in a computer magazine, and decides to download and install the utility on the Internet machine. Unwittingly, she also installs the BO server application, leaving the computer open to intrusion.
- Rather than go to the help desk, a user asks their friend to help sort out their problems. Together they manage to corrupt the hard drive. I have seen this happen frequently.
- A floppy disk was taken home by a user and used to copy some documents for his son who was at university. Later, the user remembered that the floppy disk contained some confidential documents.
- And finally, I promise you this actually happened: after coming back from the pub one Friday afternoon, a user tried to format a floppy disk but instead managed to format his hard disk by mistake.

All the examples above are ways in which security can be breached from within an organization by users' ignorance alone (remember Security includes Integrity, Availability and Confidentiality). With just a little inclination, though, the user will find that with the right tools and a little knowledge, some more interesting cracking can be undertaken. Users have a good knowledge of the network system, such as what the operating system is, what the IP addresses of various parts of the network are, etc. Moreover, users already have direct access to the system and don't have to waste time trying to gain access, they already have a valid account and a password they can use! Perhaps this is another reason why users are seen as the predominate source for security breaches.

3.3 Power supply failure

Power supply failure was found to be one of the main risks to a secure network, yet, paradoxically, is also one of the easiest risks to deal with by way of mitigating action. Some contingency is already taken care of in some cases. Network servers, for example, are designed for resilience and often have two power supplies built into the case. Therefore, in the event of one of the supplies failing due to a localized problem, such as a blown fuse, continuity is still maintained by the built-in redundancy of the second power supply.

Of course, such duplication does not prevent the server from going down in the event of a total power failure. For that reason, many businesses make use of an uninterruptible power supply, or UPS. A UPS provides a backup electricity supply to the network equipment in the event of a power cut occurring, ideally with there being no discernible transition from mains to backup which might cause momentary failure of equipment.

There are many types of UPS. Some are localized stand-by units, providing UPS services to a single computer, others are distributed throughout an entire building, reliant upon a generator to provide the electricity. But, given the relatively low cost of UPS units, particularly the stand-by units, when compared to the cost of network downtime or the risk of data loss due to a power cut, there can really be little justification in purchasing one for the server at least. Casual investigation on the Internet revealed that backup UPS units are available for just a few hundred pounds sterling. Buy a UPS!

Case Study – Power failures

Power supply failure can occur in various ways. Even with a UPS in place, continuity of power supply is not always guaranteed, particularly if there are problems with the existing mains supply. As the following cases indicate, you can still have problems even if you have your UPS in place! Power supply issues should be addressed with the greatest urgency.

- One room I once worked in had an intermittent problem in that the mains supply could cope with the ongoing power supply required by the relatively small number of PCs situated within, except for the sudden surge in power that occurred when the PCs were first turned on. Now and then, if the PCs were fired upon within a few seconds of each other, the power drawn would be enough to trip the fuses in the main supply board and cause a power cut in the whole area where the room was situated. The short-term answer was to stagger the turning on of the PCs, but the longer-term answer would be to investigate the loading on the mains and remedy accordingly.

- A similar but rather more serious problem reported in the press was that of the loss of a £400 000 computer by the Scottish Qualification Authority. The computer was wrongly wired to the electricity supply, by a contractor, who was thought to have plugged the computer into a high-voltage supply instead of the usual 240 mains. The resultant power surge destroyed the computer. Although insured for the loss, there was not enough time to replace the machine before the deadline for producing examination results that year.

- Finally, be sure that if you have a UPS that you are actually plugging your equipment into the appropriate supply. I know of one case where a user noticed that his computer had shut down in a power cut whereas his colleagues were able to carry on working. Only after a few occurrences of this did the user realize that he had actually not got his computer plugged into the UPS provided mains circuit, clearly indicated by the red plug sockets on the wall! This can be taken to extremes. Ensure that kettles, printers, and other non-essentials are not plugged into the UPS supply, or the supply will be drained quickly.

3.4 Viruses and Trojans

The computer virus is a security threat that most network administrators, if not most users, are familiar with, being aware generally of the damage that viruses can cause and the ways in which viruses can be transmitted. Due to the increasing ease with which viruses can propagate and the continued ingenuity shown by those who write viruses, however, some review of this risk would be prudent in many cases.

A virus can be described as a program that is executed on a host computer, cause some modification to the computer unknown to the user, and then copy itself by some means to other computers, without any intervention by users themselves.

When the program is executed, the user may be well aware that virus infection has occurred as the computer may be acting strangely or may cease to function at all due to disk or data corruption. Sometimes, though, the virus may execute and make no presence felt at all. These more discrete types of virus are rare, though, as usually one of the aims of virus creators is to cause disruption. The process whereby the virus is unwittingly 'installed' on a computer is often termed infection.

The pathology of virus infection has changed over time. Older viruses would often undergo a lifecycle that required the virus to occupy a particular file on a disk drive, be it the hard disk or a floppy disk. Transmission would then occur by an infected file being copied onto a new disk, such as your colleague's floppy disk, which would then infect a new computer when the host file is executed. Alternatively, the Master Boot Record of a disk might be occupied so that an infected computer will boot the virus into memory, the virus will then reside on the computer, taking advantage of any floppy disk activity in order to propagate. Thus, in both cases, the portability provided by the floppy disk offers a suitable means of transmission enabling the virus to spread. In such a way, a virus could easily spread through an office in days.

Newer viruses, though, can easily spread across the entire world in hours. This is because virus pathology has now changed, so that the main route of infection is client/server network applications. The Internet is therefore the ideal medium for virus propagation. Other aspects of the pathology of viruses are also changing, to take advantage of recent developments in software and networks.

Viruses are no longer restricted to computers running Microsoft DOS or Windows. Although for many years, viruses were indeed restricted to these operating systems, there are now reports concerning viruses for Linux that can also be compiled to run on other versions of Unix.

Viruses can now also be propagated by email. Again, a few years ago, this was not the case, despite the many chain mail 'warnings' that often circulated warning users not to open email messages with certain subject headings; these were just hoaxes. Now, though, due to the ability of many email client applications able to send and receive email with attachments that are executed on opening, such as VBScript or ActiveX attachments, spurious code can be included. The Melissa virus is a case in point here.

Virus protection software will not give you one hundred per cent complete protection against viruses. This was also demonstrated by the rapid propagation of the Melissa virus. Virus protection software is only as good as the latest update that has been installed. I know from experience that in some instances virus protection software can often be years out of date. This is worse than having no protection at all, as a false sense of security is provided to users.

Case Study – Viruses

Many people still imagine viruses as they were in the old days when symptoms of virus infection included characters on the command line display to start 'snowing' down the screen or a wiped hard drive. Recent high profile viruses have behaved in rather different ways.

- The Melissa virus was an instance of a macro virus that infected Microsoft Word 97 documents and templates, and used Microsoft Outlook for propagation. The virus was first posted to Usenet news groups on 26 March, 1999. Infection results in email being sent to 50 recipients picked from the user's address book with the subject 'Important Message From' and with the message text 'Here is that document you asked for ... don't show anyone else ;-)'. A document is enclosed which contains a list of pornographic websites.
- The virus known as 'I Love You' also infected hosts by email and replaced various computer files on the host's hard drive. The virus sends copies of itself using Microsoft Outlook to all the addresses included in the address book. The virus will then attempt to retrieve passwords from the host computer which are then sent to a third party using email.
- Yet another virus, the SirCam virus, also propagates by sending itself, together with local documents from the host computer, to other users whose email addresses are found on the host. The main problem caused by this virus is the overloading of the corporate email system. According to reports from Reuters, a Ukrainian website said that secret documents from the administration of President Leonid Kuchma had been received, which included a travel itinerary during independence celebrations. This type of embarrassment is caused because SirCam sends random document files.
- One problem associated with viruses is the frequent emails that are sent by hoaxsters and then forwarded by well-intentioned people to their friends and colleagues. This leads to a chain email type of phenomenon, which while not so damaging as an actual virus can cause some diversion from real occurrences

and also waste time. On a more serious note, some of these 'warnings' have taken a new appearance. A system administrator working for a government department received an email that urged him to check his hard drive for a certain file that might indicate virus infection. If the file was present, so the email read, the user should delete the file to prevent the virus spreading. In fact the email was malicious and the file being referred to was a critical system file. Fortunately the system administrator did not forward the email, and instead deleted the message, the best policy for such 'virus warnings'.

3.4.1 Trojans

Trojans are often associated with viruses, perhaps because like viruses Trojans are often introduced unwittingly to a computer. Then, unknown to the user, the Trojan performs some actions that are most likely detrimental to the computer's integrity or security. Trojans are introduced to the host computer by inclusion of the Trojan within a legitimate third party application or the inclusion of an 'undocumented feature' deliberately by the author of an *apparently* legitimate application.

Perhaps a subtle distinction between a Trojan and a virus can be made. Whereas a virus will usually perform wantonly destructive or dehabilitating actions, a Trojan on the other hand will usually perform actions discreetly and surreptitiously. Typical Trojan actions may be to open up unauthorized network connections, or copy and steal a password file.

There are DIY Trojan kits available for some of the better known cracker tools. The Cult of the Dead Cow, for example, has made an application available that appends the server side of Back Orifice within any legitimate application. This Trojan can then be introduced to an unwitting user, who will execute the application and then cause the Trojan to be activated. Unless adequate protection is installed on the infected computer, the user will be none the wiser.

3.4.2 Preventative action

To reduce the risk of infection by viruses, a number of measures can be taken.

- Remove floppy disk drives. Although not a strong feature of modern viruses' pathology, the floppy disk is no longer a requirement of any business that has networked computers.
- Control the download of software from the Internet. Educate

users about the desirability of downloading software from untrusted sources.

• Control email attachments by either preventing their use through policy (difficult) or use a content scanner that can detect viruses contained within attachments as email enters your network (easier).

• Install virus protection software on your networked computers. The downside to this is that virus protection software can incur a moderate overhead on the operational speed of a computer.

Note that the detection of viruses or Trojans with detection software is never foolproof. Whenever a new virus type is created, there needs to be an update to the detection software if that virus is to be detected. Do not get lulled into a false sense of security by having out-of-date virus detection software.

3.5 Denial of service

A denial of service is where a remote host computer or network is disabled, so that networked services are no longer able to function. Denial of service attacks are deliberate attempts to cause such an occurrence. There are many tools to facilitate these attacks which are available from the Internet. Because they can be launched at a distance, tracing the culprit is difficult, and the attack might also be used as a precursor or diversion to hide other activity such as intrusion. On the other hand, denial of service attacks are immediately visible, being readily apparent as soon as the associated network services are lost.

The consequences of a denial of service depend on the nature of the service being provided, but often there is a loss of productivity and therefore an increase in overhead costs. The cost to the organization affected by the denial of service can be immeasurable if the server is public facing and is part of the organization's commercial activity. Imagine the consequences if the Web servers at a major ecommerce site were halted by a denial of service attack.

Case study – Yahoo denial of service

During early February 2000, Yahoo, one of the most popular sites on the Web, was the target of a concerted attack that resulted in the website being unavailable for a few hours. The attack was a co-ordinated effort, which was thought to have originated from various locations on the Web. One of the routers that handles traffic designated for the Yahoo website was flooded with so much traffic that the router was unable to cope. The attack was only able to be rebuffed by the use of traffic filtering that removed hostile traffic prior to reaching the targeted router.

The attack was launched by the crackers only after they had 'taken over' various other hosts connected to the Internet, forcing the hosts to send traffic to the Yahoo website. Such an attack would require considerable resources, i.e. the number of hosts taken over must have been large. The service collapse affected millions of users, but although costly in terms of the lost access there was no corruption of the host file systems nor was user data damaged. Other targets of this sort of attack have included the FBI website, the website of the online auctioneer eBay, and the online retailer amazon.com.

Because many of these attacks work by exploiting inherent design weaknesses in the operating system or server software, the only viable means of prevention for many is to install updates to the software in the form of patches or hot fixes.

Denial of service attacks can be caused in many different ways, but not all denial of service incidents are due to attacks by malicious users. For instance, a server hard drive that runs out of free space will cause the server to crash. For this reason, system administrators should be sure to delete unwanted files, following backup, and take care that users are given quotas of file space for work, email, etc. Furthermore, badly written software can also cause services to be denied, such as in the case of network *Doom* which flooded networks to capacity when used.

3.6 Intrusion and unauthorized access

Intrusion occurs when someone gains unauthorized entry to your network system, using whatever means available, either from within your corporate network, or from outside using the Internet or some other means. The consequences of the intrusion depend largely on the actions taken by the intruder once they have gained access, and on the value of the data or network services that are visible to the intruder and on any disruptive actions taken.

Whereas denial of service attacks are readily evident due to the disruption caused, by their very nature incidents of intrusion are less noticeable. Most likely, if you actually notice an intruder present within your system, a lot of damage to the network's integrity may already have been done. Account details, including passwords, may have been stolen, the system administrator's account compromised and data may have been copied and siphoned off the network.

Whether breaking into a public facing server, such as a Web server, or a computer that is part of a private network, the actual task of breaking into a network system is often carried out incrementally over a period of time. To use the metaphor of breaking into a house, a cracker will often case out the target computer, taking note of access points and any weaknesses that might enable easy entry. Having gained access, once inside the cracker will then explore the file system to see what is available. Make no mistake, like a good cat burglar, the experienced intruder will make no disturbance, will cover his tracks, and will pass unnoticed.

The process can be summarized as follows:

- Establish as much information as possible about the target computer, such as IP address, domain names, associated hosts sharing the same network, the operating system and server software being used, including major and minor version numbers. Identify which ports appear to be open, and associate each port with a particular service application.
- A denial of service attack may be launched at this point, by searching the Internet for known vulnerabilities of various services found on the computer.
- With a list of default accounts and passwords for each service application running on the computer, an attempt will be made to gain access to the default named accounts. Ideally, administrative access will be obtained, but a user account will often give sufficient privilege to move around the file system. Continued use by system administrators of default passwords following installation of server software is one of the main ways by which access can be gained by unauthorized parties. There are comprehensive lists of default passwords available from the Internet. Default passwords are like having no password at all!
- Alternatively, the cracker will attempt to log on to suspected user accounts relying on some inside knowledge and the fact that many people do not use particularly strong password protection. Alongside default passwords, use of weak or easy to remember passwords represents a severe weakness to the integrity of a network computer.
- If a user account has been obtained, then an attempt will be made to leverage that limited access and to break into or create an administrative account providing full access to the

computer. This may be done by using password cracking methods, by using vulnerabilities in system utilities that are available to users, or by using a purpose written utility.

- Once administrative access is obtained, the cracker will most likely attempt to cover their tracks by deleting or overwriting log files. They may also use engineered versions of system utilities that, while masquerading as legitimate versions, are also designed to carry out monitoring activities and intelligence gathering. Information may be copied, and easy access routes created so that subsequent access to the system is facilitated. Cracking tools, such as password crackers or network monitors, may be set up to run in the background consuming resources.

- Once the activities are completed, the cracker will remove as much evidence of their ongoing presence as possible, and will then leave the system again with the administrator usually being none the wiser that any unauthorized access has taken place. Many crackers claim not to be deliberately destructive.

3.6.1 Preventative measures

The single most important measure that can be made against intrusion is to ensure that passwords are sufficiently strong to stand up to repeated attempts to gain access. Coupled with strong passwords, there should be an automatic locking of accounts after a small number of unsuccessful attempts to log on to the account.

There are various utilities that are available for download from the Internet that enable you to some extent to monitor the goings-on on your system. Many of these tools are available for Unix platforms, but this is probably due to the differing nature of the threat of intrusion with regard to Windows and Unix systems. There is not so much capacity to remotely enter an NT server and execute commands that run on that server, as there is in a Unix system.

3.7 Use for unauthorized purposes

Use for unauthorized purposes is a rather broad description of various instances of security breaches that might occur within a network. At the most trivial end of the spectrum, printing out a child's homework on the colour laser printer at work may be counted as unauthorized use. There is the installation and subsequent use of unauthorized software, such as games or shareware applications from cover discs. Then comes the serious abuse, such as the use of some of the tools that are discussed in the next chapter. There is the use of computers in a way that might constitute the breach of company policy, for instance using the Internet to check on one's online share portfolio. At the most serious end of the scale is the unauthorized use that might also embrace actions that could lead to infringement of the law, such as the use of a computer in order to gain unauthorized access to another computer on the Internet.

Case Study – Anyone for cricket?

Instances of unauthorized use are wide and varied, but perhaps the most novel situation was that told to me by a system administrator from a financial institution. For some time, he had been investigating a number of PCs that would intermittently crash for no apparent reason. All the software appeared to be fine. Close investigation of the rear of the PC revealed that there appeared to be an extra card device installed in each of the problem PCs. This turned out to be a television card that had been installed by the users into their PCs so that they could watch the cricket during their working day! This 'upgrade' caused some unexpected system conflicts.

3.7.1 Can 'unauthorized use' be prevented?

In a word, no. Trivial instances of unauthorized use will always occur. Parents will always be tempted to print out homework for their children. But there are ways in which unauthorized use can be made rather more difficult, and use can be monitored rather more overtly than is often the case in many organizations.

But, prevention is always better then retrospective detection. To this end, there are measures that can be taken to reduce the ease with which computers can be used for purposes other than work, such as disabling the rights of ordinary user accounts to install software, and defining what constitutes unauthorized use within your organization. These measures should be documented within your security policy. Inform users that monitoring of their activities is entirely possible, and from time to time examine the multitude of logs that are generated by servers to check for possible instances of misuse.

Users need to be educated about what constitutes acceptable use. They are often genuinely unaware of the ease with which their actions can be monitored. Informing them of a minor infringement might be better than waiting to catch them committing a really serious act of misuse. Acceptable use is discussed in more detail in Chapter 8.

3.8 Infringements of various legal Acts

For many years, the use of computer and information systems was unregulated by law. As a consequence, users, both at home and in the workplace, were able to behave in a way that these days would render them liable to prosecution. Since the mid-1980s, with the introduction of the Data Protection Act 1984, and then subsequently the Computer Misuse Act, the situation has changed. Now, individuals and businesses may find themselves breaking the law without ever being aware of the fact, through misuse of data gathered from a website, for instance. For an individual accused of breaking the law, the consequences can be serious and may result subsequently in loss of their job in addition to any legal penalties imposed by the courts. For an organization found to be in breach of the law, at the very least their reputation will be damaged.

Either way, for a business to be found to have infringed one of the many Acts that legislate computer use, the net result will be financial expense borne as a result of loss of business, legal expenses, costs, and perhaps a fine. If you are in any doubt as to the seriousness and impact of this risk, then consider the following.

When an employee sent just one email, which was found subsequently to be libellous, Norwich Union was fined £450 000. Yet, several years after that precedent was sent, organizations either permit or turn a blind eye to potentially unlawful use of email, or worse still are completely ignorant of the fact that carelessly composed or casually used email can lead to all sorts of legal troubles. A review of the legal issues regarding network and computer use is contained in Chapter 5, and is useful reading before acceptable use is examined.

3.9 Disasters and public disorder

Most organizations are unlikely to be affected by disaster or public disorder, both being relatively scarce scenarios. But, for any business that has been subjected to any disaster or an incident of public disorder, the costs can be devastating, resulting even in closure of the business. The main reason for subsequent closure is the lack of ability of the business to continue operating when business premises and operating infrastructure are lost, even if that loss is only temporary. Consider what might happen if, for instance, there were extensive floods that caused a great part of your building to be feet deep in water. Of course, the building would be unusable. For many businesses, one of the main parts of operational infrastructure is the computer network. Like all other electrical equipment, the flood would render the network inoperative. In such a position businesses are faced with a choice: either cease operation for the duration of the disaster or set up temporary operational space in premises elsewhere.

Desks and chairs are often easy to come by, telephones may even be rerouted to provide a means of continued contact with customers and the supply chain. Even computers and network hardware are relatively easy to come by. But difficulties arise when an attempt is made to migrate the computer network to the temporary premises, so that functionality and data can be made available as soon as possible, in order that the discontinuity to the business is minimized.

The facilitation and management of such a migration is the reason that many businesses have business continuity plans in place which provide a course of mitigation should a disaster or public disorder take place. Business continuity plans contain actions and directives that are initiated when disaster strikes, and in particular address the provision of alternative premises, network hardware, and data.

The main issue that business must tackle in addressing business continuity is the definition, assessment and qualification of the risks involved, and the subsequent benefit cost calculation required in order to justify the cost incurred through maintaining a business continuity plan. In short, can your business afford to be without access to the computer network for more than a few minutes at a time? For some businesses, the answer is 'yes'. For others, the answer is 'no', and the costs incurred due to discontinuity of network availability could be millions of pounds for every minute of downtime, particularly with reference to the finance sector. Business continuity is discussed in Chapter 9.

Disasters happen

Disasters are not a remote possibility, far removed from everyday life. For those who think that disaster always happens to other people, then mull over the damage caused by the flooding that occurred in many parts of the UK during the early part of 2001.

Some cities experienced flooding on a scale that was unprecedented in living memory. York city centre was flooded, in the worst case of flooding for circa 400 years. Water was 18 feet higher than normal and peaked at one point just two inches below defences. The city was protected with thousands of sandbags laid by the emergency services and the army, and more than three thousand people were made homeless.

Floods also impact on transport infrastructure, which could impact an otherwise unaffected business by the absence of staff who are unable to travel to work. At the time of the floods, Railtrack had planned to repair 35 km of track. The water, together with the backlog of work, placed a burden on the already overloaded rail network. Roads become impassable, particularly for those living in rural areas.

As a result of the prevalent flooding that occurred, not just in York but throughout the country, the government announced that money will be devoted to researching the possible link between recently observed global warming and the current floods. 'Severe flooding could become more common as a result of global warming', predicted John Prescott, Deputy Prime Minister.

3.10 Breach of confidentiality of data

This threat is associated with another of the threats addressed earlier, unauthorized access to a computer system, and lies at the core of the three principles of secure networks, i.e. availability, integrity, and confidentiality. For many system administrators, therefore, one of the worst instances of security breach could be the breach of confidentiality of data. Such a breach could result in one or more of the following:

- Loss of competitive advantage.
- Loss of reputation.
- Loss of business.
- Lack of compliance with legal obligation, should personal data be compromised, for instance.

There are many and varied ways in which data is protected. Measures include account and password control, correct configuration of server software, encryption of data both in transit and in storage, and measures to protect against accidental divulgence to third parties. Within the business sector in particular, the threat of confidentiality being breached should be taken seriously, and is likely to be of increasing relevance. Already, there are cases where industrial intelligence gathering, orchestrated by blue chip businesses against competitors, has got out of hand and resulted in some embarrassing cases of theft coming to light. As more documentation is available in electronic format, there will in many cases be no need to stuff photocopied papers in a briefcase, just a couple of floppy disks instead, or better still just attach a few documents to an email.

The cost of confidentiality breaches

The 2000 CSI/FBI computer survey, conducted in the United States, reports that the theft of proprietary information has cost over $66 million. As in previous years, this was the most costly security breach found by this particular survey.

Cases of confidentiality being breached on the Web are commonplace, often involving credit card details. In one such instance, again reported on the 2000 CSI/FBI survey, VISA International estimated that the potential cost of recovering all compromised credit cards would amount to up to $125 million for just one incident! Apart from the financial costs, though, is the loss of confidence that is brought about by confidentiality breaches. Right or wrong, consumers are nervous about using their credit cards on the Web because they fear their card data will not remain confidential.

3.11 Review

- The threats to a secure network include users, viruses, power failure, denial of service attacks, unauthorized access, breach of confidentiality of data, lack of legal compliance, disasters.
- Of these threats, the main threats to network security come from user operator error, viruses, and interruption to the power supply.
- Virus detection software should be installed on workstation computers.

- Software updates should be applied to remove potential vulnerabilities that could be exploited by third parties to launch a denial of service attack or to gain unauthorized access.
- Appropriate use of passwords will make unauthorized access more difficult.
- The biggest threat to the secure network comes from within your organization, with circa 60 per cent of all security breaches originating from inside an organization.
- A policy should be defined in order that users can be clear about what constitutes acceptable use.
- Organizations are being placed under increased legal obligation, with the revised Data Protection Act being just one recent instance of where many were ignorant of changes to the law. The acceptable use policy should be drawn up only following consideration of the appropriate legal framework.
- Organizations should have a disaster recovery and business continuity plan to mitigate the effects of unforeseen occurrences.
- An appropriate level of data confidentiality is pivotal to network security.

3.12 To do

3.12.1 Start to determine the prevalence of various types of security breach

- Start an incident book that catalogues the instances of security breaches within your organization. The book will help to identify areas where attention should be focused when conducting the risk assessment and when documenting the security policy.
- You need to establish which breaches to record. Use the types of breach discussed in this chapter as a starting point, or examine some of the surveys referenced in Chapter 1 for additional instances of security breach.
- For each breach, try to establish a realistic estimate of the cost incurred by the breach including:
  1. Productivity loss or revenue loss due to the breach occurring
  2. Cost of rectifying the situation
  3. The cost of any adverse effects such as damage to reputation
- Ensure that your colleagues and users are aware of this cataloguing activity and encourage open and honest reporting in order to gain an accurate representative survey.

- Use the results of the survey to identify areas of network security to address and remedy.
- Use the costs as a powerful argument to make the case for taking network security seriously in your organization.

4 Tools of the trade

Consider that at one of the largest technology companies, where policy required that passwords exceed 8 characters, mix cases, and include numbers or symbols L0phtCrack cracked 18% of the passwords in 10 minutes, 90% of the passwords were recovered within 48 hours on a Pentium II/300.

(@stake, distributors of L0phtCrack)

4.1 Introduction

This chapter contains a review of some of the various software tools that anyone interested in network security should be familiar with. Some of these tools are already part of the operating system, others are readily available from the Internet. At this point some readers might question the wisdom of including discussion on software tools that can have potentially undesirable consequences. Well, I would argue that anyone dealing with network security should not only be aware of these tools, but should also try some out, and be aware of the results these tools might generate when used against their own network. I would rather find out myself that 90 per cent of my users' passwords are woefully inadequate before someone else finds out. Moreover, if anyone really wants to find out about these tools all they need to do is go to an Internet search engine or directory. Go to your favourite search engine and see what references you can find, you will most likely be amazed! Now consider that anyone in your organization might already have been to those very same websites, and already have downloaded the applications and 'tested' them on your network!

4.2 Tools that come with your operating system

A lot of information about a network can be derived by using the various utilities available from the command line prompt, either from the Windows command prompt or from the Unix shell. Use of these utilities is similar within each operating system, but there are sometimes slight differences in syntax. In any case, the help files can be consulted should difficulties arise.

4.2.1 Ping

Ping is a useful tool for system administrators, often used to verify the presence of a connection to a remote host and to confirm that the network is functioning correctly. The ping utility sends out small data packets to the remote host, and then listens for a response from that host, thus indicating that the network connection is present. Data packets are sent in the form of ICMP datagrams, containing an IP and an ICMP header and then some arbitrary amount of padding data. The size of the padding data packet can be set in the command switches, but is usually set to a default of 32 or 64 bytes depending on which operating system or version of ping is being used.

The ping command is easy to use. At the command prompt, just type ping followed by the IP address or domain name of the destination host computer. When the ping packet is received by the remote host, the packet is returned to provide confirmation of an open route. In this way, for example, ping can be used to check that each computer on a network is able to send and receive network traffic (Figure 4.1).

Be aware that networks can very easily be scoped out from a distance by using ping. Some firewalls do not prevent ICMP ping requests from passing through into a secure network, even though TCP/IP traffic is filtered. This fact is not widely appreciated. In order to ascertain the presence of various computers or other hardware on a network, a series of IP addresses can be systematically pinged. If the address is being used, a response will be received confirming the existence of a computer or some other hardware at that address. There are tools available that can automate this process. The user can just enter a range of IP addresses into the tool, and after a while, a list of live IP addresses is returned.

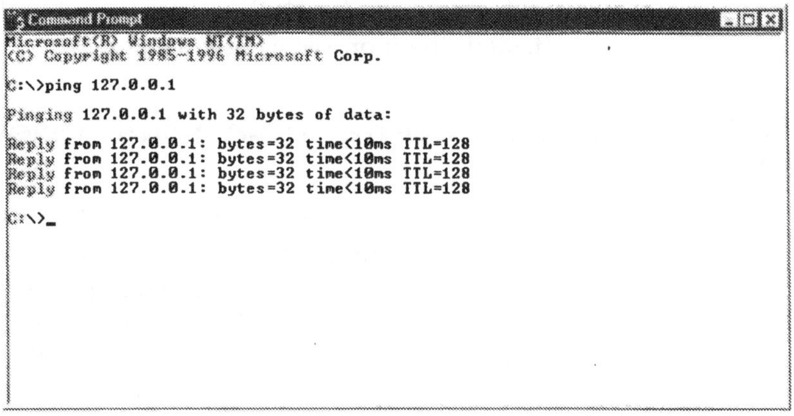

Figure 4.1
The ping command

4.2.2 Telnet client

Telnet clients can be found within most out-of-the-box installations of network operating systems including Unix and Windows. In operation telnet enables a user to connect to another host computer, with an appropriate account and password. Once authenticated, the user can then interact with the host, issuing commands remotely. In practice, this means that an administrator can connect to various networked computers, such as Web servers, and perform administrative tasks remotely.

Telnet is easy to use, from the command line prompt in Unix or from the command shell in Windows, type the command 'telnet' followed by the IP address or the domain name of the remote computer you want to connect to. The default listening port for a telnet server is port 23, and accordingly this is the default port to which the telnet client sends requests to the remote host.

There is, however, a little known switch for the telnet command which allows a user to connect to any other port on the remote host, instead of the default port 23. To connect telnet to an alternative port, rather than the default port 23, simply type the alternative port number after the IP address or domain name of the remote host. For instance, the command telnet 127.0.0.1 13 would connect to port 13 on your own computer. The response from port 13 is the day and time. Another port that could be connected to is port 7, which is an echo port. This sends an echo of all the data that is sent to it. Other ports that can be connected to are the SMTP port 25, the NNTP port 119, and the HTTP port 80. In this way, server applications can easily be investigated.

All well and good, but where does this lead? Well, a command issued by the user through the telnet client will usually provoke a response from the server application being queried. This response, which is shown in the telnet client screen (Figure 4.2), often includes the name of the server application, the release number, and other host specific information. This information can be very useful to anyone wishing to gain access to or otherwise disrupt your network.

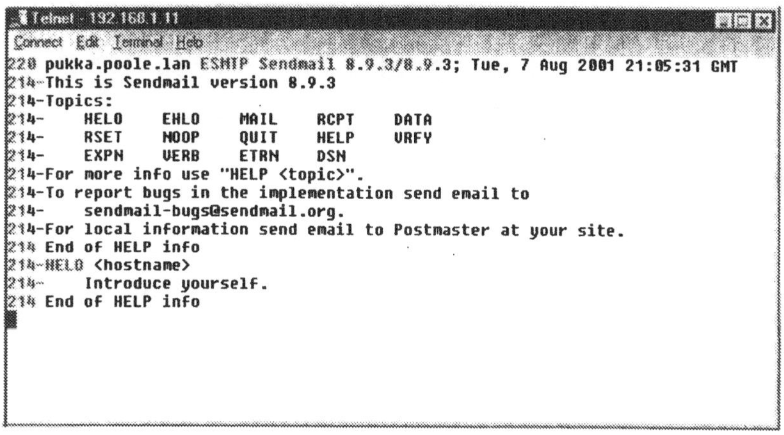

Figure 4.2
Telnet client screen

4.2.3 Netstat

The netstat tool is included within Microsoft Windows, and also within many Unix distributions, including Linux. The netstat command provides a report on all current network connections and additional networking information. This information can be updated in real time to provide an ongoing display of network activity.

The value of netstat to an administrator is clear. By running the utility there is a ready facility to view connections to the network server in real time. Getting in the habit of examining the output from netstat now and then will enable system administrators to become accustomed to what is 'normal' network behaviour (Figure 4.3).

The Windows netstat utility displays protocol statistics and current TCP/IP network connections for the computer, and includes information on the remote IP addresses connected, the port number that is being used, and also the protocol being used over the connection. The netstat utility is used from within the command shell, just type netstat then return. Several command

```
Command Prompt                                                    _ □ X
    Proto   Local Address           Foreign Address         State
    TCP     peach:1025              localhost:1026          ESTABLISHED
    TCP     peach:1026              localhost:1025          ESTABLISHED

C:\>netstat

Active Connections

    Proto   Local Address           Foreign Address         State
    TCP     peach:1025              localhost:1026          ESTABLISHED
    TCP     peach:1026              localhost:1025          ESTABLISHED
    TCP     peach:1171              www.google.com:80       ESTABLISHED

C:\>netstat

Active Connections

    Proto   Local Address           Foreign Address         State
    TCP     peach:1025              localhost:1026          ESTABLISHED
    TCP     peach:1026              localhost:1025          ESTABLISHED
    TCP     peach:1174              216.239.37.106:80       ESTABLISHED
    TCP     peach:1175              216.239.37.106:80       ESTABLISHED

C:\>
```

Figure 4.3
The Windows netstat utility

switches are available, these are shown in the netstat help file, accessed from the Windows help index.

The Unix netstat utility is accessed from the Unix command shell, again just type netstat then return. The Unix manual page contains detailed coverage of the utility, just type man netstat for more information.

4.2.4 ipconfig

On Microsoft Windows NT and Windows 2000 computers, the network settings are usually hidden from view unless the administrative account is being used. There is another small utility, ipconfig, that will reveal TCP/IP network information not just to the administrator account but to all accounts. The ipconfig utility is used from within the command shell, with the most useful form of the command being ipconfig /all. This displays TCP/IP networking information for each network adapter used in the computer, including the DHCP information if dynamic IP numbers are being allocated.

The risks incurred by allowing normal user accounts to obtain this sort of information are not huge. The benefits to the administrator of the command are that all the important information can be viewed in one easy to read display, providing an instant digest of the network information for each computer (Figure 4.4).

There is a similar utility for Unix systems, the ifconfig utility, usually available to the root administrative user only. When used without command switches, TCP/IP information for each

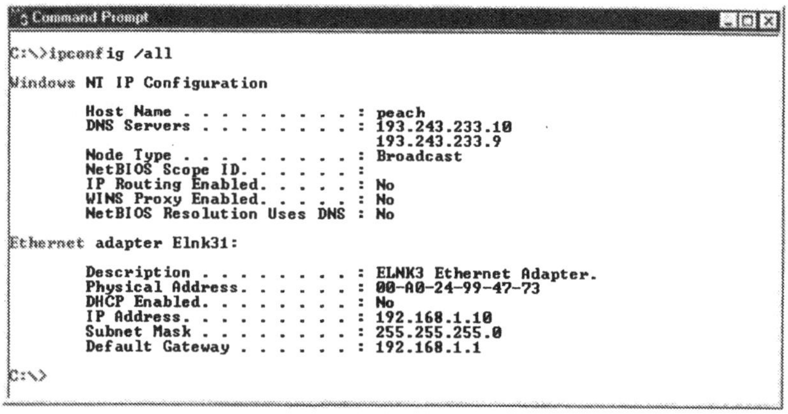

Figure 4.4
The Windows ipconfig utility

network adapter is displayed. With appropriate switches, the command can also be used to configure network adapters.

4.2.5 Event Viewer

Windows contains a comprehensive system logging tool that offers the audit trail for all events that have taken place on the system, called Event Viewer. There are three categories of event that can be recorded: system, security and application. The extent to which events are logged can be determined by the system administrator. Of most interest here is the security event logger, which records events that might be security breaches. This might include, for instance, attempts to log in to an account or attempts to open folders by an account that has insufficient privilege (Figure 4.5).

4.2.6 Unix system logs

Unix server applications write a record of events to log files, which are usually in plain text format. Using a text editor, the system administrator can then examine these log files. The system logs are usually kept in a location such as /var/logs, and the files are written to by the background daemons or services that are being run, such as the syslogd daemon which monitors and receives incoming log messages which are started at boot time (Figure 4.6). There are other system monitoring files that are written by Web servers such as Apache, and by SMB servers such as Samba.

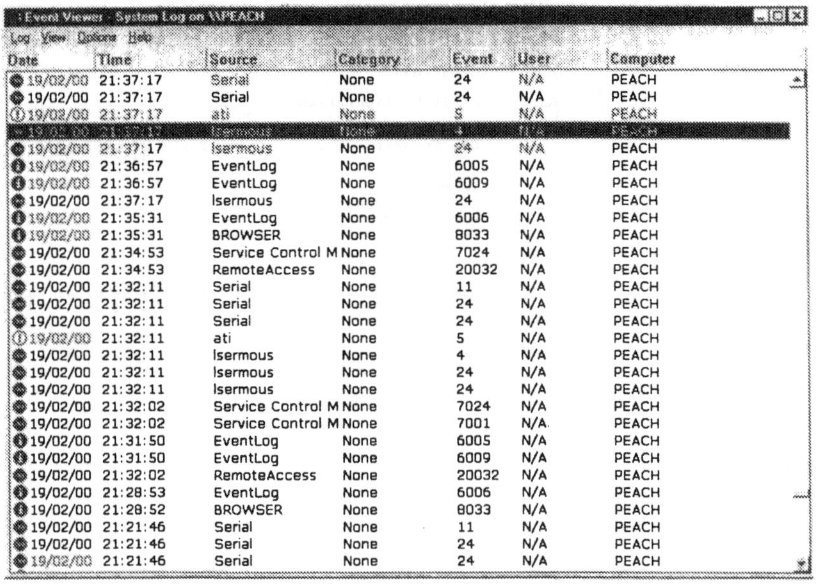

Figure 4.5
Event Viewer

Logs are kept of system usage, and use of the Unix system can be monitored by two commands, who and last. Both commands are issued at the command shell. The who command displays a list of users logged in at the time the command is issued. The last command displays a list of all the user account activity history, in terms of account log in and logging out. Use this with care, because the command displays all users who have ever logged on! Issuing the command with a numerical switch will show the activity for the last *n* users, for example last -5 shows the last five users.

4.3 Port scanners

Now, we move onto a more sophisticated tool, the port scanner. This is a very useful tool for anyone, i.e. a cracker, interested in scoping out a particular computer. Recall that in Chapter 2 we discussed services and protocols and learnt that each network service listens on a dedicated and fixed port for incoming requests. A Web server, for example, using HTTP will listen for incoming traffic on port 80 by default, while an email server using SMTP will listen on port 25.

Because the allocation of port numbers is standardized, if there was a way of determining which ports were open and

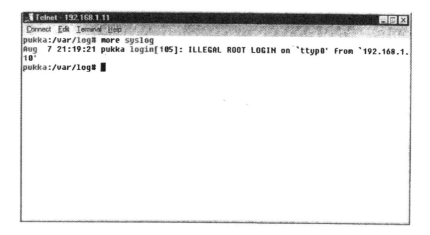

Figure 4.6
Syslogd log file output

listening on a remote host, then we would be able to build up a pretty good idea of what service applications are running on a remote host. We could even telnet to those ports in an attempt to identify which particular version of the application software is running those services, by attempting to elicit a response within the telnet client. Then, particular vulnerabilities associated with the server application could be identified (Figure 4.7).

The port scanner can remotely scan a target host, determine which ports are open, and therefore provide all the information we require, concerning which services are likely to be running. If a cracker was to scan a computer and find that among others, port 80 was open and receiving traffic, then most likely that computer is acting as a Web server. Armed with this knowledge, a cracker can then telnet to port 80, elicit a response that enables the application software providing the service to be identified, usually with the major and minor release number. Then, the name of the server application software can be looked up on a list, perhaps on a list of known bugs, in order to determine a vulnerability associated with that software that could provide the means of breaching the remote host's security.

Port scanners are lightweight applications, and as such are very portable. They can easily fit onto a floppy disk, for example, and can be downloaded from the Internet very quickly. There are port scanner applications available for all the operating systems discussed above, including Unix and Windows.

As a security expert, the port scanner is a useful tool. The more ports that are left open on a computer, corresponding to

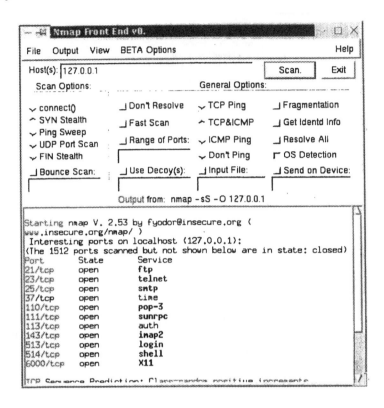

Figure 4.7
The port scanner

unattended server applications perhaps installed by default, the more leverage a would-be cracker could exert. Therefore, pointing a port scanner at a network computer might reveal that there are more ports open than you really need.

A Web server, for example, would really need port 80, and perhaps port 20/21, open by default, corresponding to HTTP and FTP services. I have seen many computers on the Internet, supposedly set up as Web servers, that are little more than out-of-the-box default installations of various operating systems. One system in particular that sticks in my mind was from a business that had clearly just used a box-fresh default Linux installation, and had practically every port under the sun open and listening for traffic. This indicated that there were some very insecure services up and running on what should have been a far more secure computer. Of course, if any of your users are seen or found to be using a port scanner, then you might wonder for what purpose they are 'evaluating' such software!

4.4 Network scanners

Network scanners are similar to port scanners, but are usually considerably larger applications and provide rather more facilities. Ostensibly, network scanners are administrative tools, but, again like port scanners, network scanners can be used by crackers to find out information about a remote host. The information provided, however, is usually far more comprehensive and specific. In short, network scanners can take a lot of the legwork out of scoping out a remote host or network.

Network scanners are pointed at a local or remote host on a network, by using the appropriate IP address. Then, they can be used to determine detailed information including which services are running, just as a port scanner can infer, and also what account names the services are running under, whether or not anonymous logins to services such as FTP are enabled, and whether authentication is required on various services. Also, the particular application used to provide each service could be ascertained.

Then, some network scanners will provide a report describing known weaknesses for each service application found on the remote server. This is done by referencing information gathered about a host against a database of associated vulnerabilities that is included with the scanner application.

All this is very potent stuff, so much so that much controversy accompanied the launch of one such scanner, called SATAN, short for Security Administrators Tool for Analysing Networks. The release of SATAN was reported extensively in the media at the time, and a great deal of adverse publicity was given to the tool. SATAN was in fact based on another tool, called COPS, short for Computer Oracle and Password System, so the concept of a network scanner was nothing new at the time. The controversy arose due to the fact that SATAN could be deployed against another host on a network, rather than just on the local host on which the tool was running.

That was all some time ago. Now, as well as SATAN, there are countless other fully fledged network scanners, including some that claim to offer stealth scanning to probe behind firewalls. Like port scanners, network scanners should be used in controlled circumstances by experienced administrators. This should be in order to ascertain what information would be divulged in the event of a third party carrying out the same activity – after all, network scanners are marketed in order to be used as the basis for tightening security. But, you should absolutely forbid anyone else on the network to use a scanner, if for no other reason than that some scanners can be quite aggressive when probing a host, and might cause some services to crash. On no account do ordinary users have any need to evaluate network scanners on the corporate network!

4.5 Denial of service device applets

Some of the most dangerous tools available are some of the specialized denial of service applets. Many of these applets exploit weaknesses in TCP/IP implementations due to the TCP/IP implementation being unable to trap nonsensical or illegal network data. These weaknesses have now been fixed in many cases, and the applets no longer have the ability to cause damage as they once had. But, they serve to illustrate the extent to which vulnerabilities, once discovered, can be exploited. One such example of the type of tool that can be downloaded is a tool called Winnuke. The Winnuke attack is a denial of service attack that relies upon the inability of Windows 95 and Windows NT to handle illegal data sent to a port. In principle any port that listens to data can be attacked, but in practice the most commonly attacked port is port 139 which is used by SMB NETBios. When sent illegal data, earlier versions of Windows 95 or NT will respond in a variety of ways, from stalling network services to a full-scale system crash. When Winnuke is directed toward a server, a denial of service is caused, as the server loses ability to send or receive any network traffic. When I first downloaded Winnuke, I was amazed at how effective this tool was at disabling remote computers, and the tool certainly provides a graphic demonstration of the ease with which denial of service attacks can be launched (Figure 4.8).

Figure 4.8
Winnuke

4.6 Email bombs

Email bombs offer yet another way of inducing a denial of service on a remote host, this time specifically aimed at hosts that run an email service, and provide an easy way to invoke denial of service. Email bombs exploit the fact that email, when received by a mail server, is stored locally on the server hard drive until such a time as the email message is downloaded by a user or in some cases until the mail is deleted by the email server administrator. If email is not deleted periodically from the server, then over time enough email could accumulate so that the hard drive is completely full, causing the server to stall.

An email bomb application is able to send a sufficiently large volume of email to a target host, which causes the mail server's hard drive capacity to be filled up very quickly. A mail bomb could be comprised of either a single very large mail message or a smaller message sent repeatedly. Some variants of this basic functionality work by tying up the mail server with connections and incoming messages simultaneously so that the service hangs with an overload.

Most mail bombs have the sender's email addresses spoofed so that the target host administrator will often have little idea of the true source of the email. In addition there are many anonymous remailers that can be used to forward the email on from the initial sender. Some tools have been written by the cracker community that enable mail bombs to be delivered more efficiently than by hand from email applications.

You might think that a cracker would require a valid email address in order to launch an email bomb, but this is not always the case. There are many mail servers on the Internet, which offer mail relaying services without any authentication taking place. This means that anyone can send mail utilizing these servers.

Latterly, there is a variation on the email bomb theme, whereby instead of sending the entire bomb payload from a single computer, the services of mailing lists on the Internet are covertly used. This is known as list linking, whereby an unsuspecting user's email account is added to a multitude of email lists, and is therefore sent a large number of emails from the list servers. These list servers are used to send email to a discussion forum or to a group of direct mail subscribers, often concentrating messages on special interest subjects, and including binary attachments to the email. Of course, mail lists can be subscribed to by hand, but there are several applets that can automate the task. As far as the target is concerned, the trouble of receiving continual email does not stop with the threat of denial of service as each email list often has to be unsubscribed by hand.

In any case, system administrators should not ignore the potential for accumulating email to cause a server to crash. Servers slowly accumulate email from redundant accounts that have not been deleted or from application email accounts that report errors through not being managed correctly. A proper user account policy of positive deletion after a user leaves the organization or of mail expiry is an important defence against accidental denial of service. Alternatively, disk quotas can limit the amount of user space allocated on a user by user basis so that the disk will not fill up entirely.

Simplistic as they sound, do not underestimate the effectiveness of email bombs in causing at least a denial of email services, or worse, a complete crash of the target computer. Remember, even a large Word or PowerPoint attachment has been known to cause some mail servers to crash!

4.7 Back Orifice and BO Y2K

Back Orifice is an interesting application that, like SATAN, created a great deal of publicity when launched. The name is a pun on the Microsoft Back Office server suite, and Back Orifice is one the highest profile cracking tools seen in recent times, and is also one of the most deceptive and comprehensive in terms of the facilities and control that the application affords to crackers.

Back Orifice is a client/server application, this architecture being perhaps Back Orifice's only weakness. For Back Orifice to work, the server component must be somehow installed on the target host. This action, however, is not as difficult as you might believe. The server can be renamed so as to appear completely innocuous, or can even be wrapped into another application such as a game or applet to create a Trojan.

Once installed, the server enables the infected computer to be comprehensively controlled by any Back Orifice client. The client can be executed on a remote computer, which could be on the same local network as the victim, or could even be on the Internet. Using the Back Orifice client, the cracker can delete files on the target computer, execute commands, start and close down services, manipulate the registry, trigger pop-up windows to appear on the target's desktop, etc.

Back Orifice originally worked on Microsoft Windows 95 computers only, but the later BO Y2K release also works with Microsoft Windows NT hosts. Fortunately, up-to-date virus detection software will scan for the presence of BO and BO Y2K, and will report an infection if the server component is found.

4.8 Password crackers

A password cracker is a powerful tool which is used by crackers and administrators alike, albeit for rather different purposes. Account passwords are usually held on a computer in some form of encrypted format. When password authentication takes place, i.e. the password is entered into the login prompt, that password is then subjected to some encryption process and compared to the password stored on file. If the two match, then the user account is authenticated and the account is then open. Clearly, if passwords are divulged there could be a breach of security.

Password crackers generally work by conducting the password encryption process offline. Automated password guesses are made, using either dictionary words or brute force random combinations of characters, and then comparing the encrypted password guesses to illegally obtained copies of the password file, or to the actual password file itself if access to that file is possible.

4.8.1 L0phtcrack (spelt with a zero)

One popular type of password cracker for Windows is L0phtcrack by L0pht Heavy Industries. Using L0phtcrack, encrypted form passwords are obtained from the registry file and the user can then execute L0phtcrack to gain access to thousands of password guesses at a time. Remember, though, that in many instances the registry file is protected from ordinary users.

As well as L0phtcrack for Windows, there are also many Unix password crackers which work on the /etc/passwd file. Cracker can work quickly and with large numbers of user accounts. In many cases, Unix passwords are protected by the shadow password scheme. Some password crackers are unable to work in such situations (Figure 4.9).

4.8.2 The value of password crackers to administrators

Passwords are valuable because they are often the first and biggest hurdle that a cracker will face in trying to gain access to a computer system. The value of passwords should not be underestimated, yet to many users passwords are a nuisance. Most

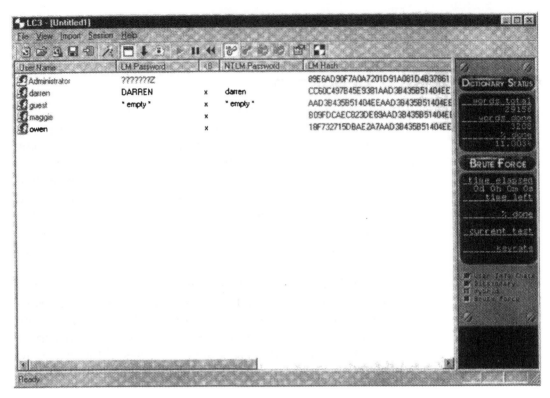

Figure 4.9
LOphtcrack

users prefer to set comparatively weak passwords, as they are seen to be easier to remember. As an administrator, however, you should know that password crackers are readily available, easy to use with little knowledge of computers required, and they are also quick to do the job in many instances.

Because users often choose passwords that are woefully weak, most password crackers make short work of them. Passwords are also the first line of defence against many instances of unauthorized access. For this reason, system administrators should run password crackers on their computers in order to assess for themselves just how weak some passwords really are. Of course, if passwords are really weak, then they can often be guessed by human intervention alone.

4.9 Network analysers

If, when you see a password cracker you are shocked into taking security more seriously, then prepare to be shocked even further. The network analyser is perhaps the daddy of all security tools, enabling anyone to eavesdrop into network traffic that originates from or is destined to the local network. Network analysers are able to intercept and decode all traffic that is routed along the network and display the contents of the traffic in an easy to use interface, and the implications of this fact are profound for anyone interested in security.

Each individual network message is displayed, including the source and destination IP addresses or domain names, the transmitting and destination port numbers, the protocol type, and the contents of each of the seven protocol layers. In practice, sniffing network traffic means that the contents of Web pages being downloaded by other network users, for instance, can be viewed. Credit card numbers can be viewed unless encryption is used, user names and passwords can be viewed if unen-

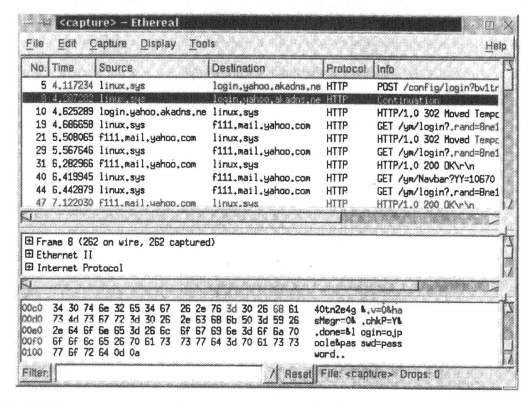

Figure 4.10
Network analyser

crypted, even if passwords are encrypted, the encrypted form can still be copied and if the encryption is weak the passwords can be cracked offline (Figure 4.10).

The network analyser relies upon the fact that network traffic is broadcast across an entire local network, rather than being directed to the particular network interface that holds the destination IP address. Therefore, for the network analyser to be deployed, appropriate TCP/IP details of the local area network must be known. If the network analyser is located on a machine that does not have the correct TCP/IP configuration, eavesdropping cannot occur.

The footprint of the analyser is fairly small, when used in a basic format, meaning that deployment is easy and inconspicuous. Also, although they used to be costly and often required proprietary hardware, these days analysers are available free of charge and are able to be installed on a standard laptop computer. This gives rise to a possible scenario whereby a cracker could plug a notebook computer into a network, leave for some period of time, and then return to retrieve the notebook and subsequently peruse the resulting captured traffic. This would be made all the easier in a network that uses DHCP, as no prior knowledge of the TCP/IP addresses would be required.

Such an occurrence would represent a serious security breach, and, if the anecdotal evidence is to be believed, has already happened in numerous instances. Then, consider the use of wireless networks, where a network analyser could intercept network traffic even from across the street! For this reason, many wireless networks are able to pass encrypted traffic. This is an option that should be turned on!

As far as network and security administrators are concerned, network analysers are invaluable, as they allow troubleshooting to be carried out very easily. As far as users are concerned, there is no reason why they should be using a network analyser at all.

4.10 File integrity scanners

After reading about all these tools that have been written in many cases to facilitate the breaking and entering of remote systems, a question you might be asking is how can you tell that an intruder has broken into your computer? Unfortunately, in many instances you may be blissfully unaware of any intrusion having taken place. Often there is no permanent damage to your system, intruders may just be utilizing your processing time for various tasks such as password cracking, or they may be using your machine as a route to other computers, the theory being that tracks may be covered by telneting through multiple computers. One of the ways in which intruders do at times leave a trail is when Trojans are introduced, masquerading as ordinary system files. This is particularly relevant to Unix systems, where many file systems' commands are available in source code format and can be recompiled in modified form. A system administrator might feel more comfortable knowing whether or not certain files have in fact been tampered with or substituted, and there are many file integrity scanners that can help with this. One of these is called Tripwire.

4.10.1 Tripwire

Tripwire is a software tool that checks file and directory integrity in case of alteration or substitution. Information about files is stored in a database and after some time the database entries for the files can be compared to the current versions of the files. Any differences are logged and the administrator can then act accordingly. In this way important system files can be monitored for changes by unauthorized users. Tripwire is available from ftp://info.cert.org/pub/tools/tripwire/.

4.11 Network monitoring tools

There are various utilities that are available – some already installed on your operating system, others available for download from the Internet – that enable you to monitor to some extent the network connections and activity taking place on your system. Many of these tools are available for Unix and Microsoft Windows operating systems. Two of these for Unix systems are listed below. Certainly, the utilities that are already installed with your operating system should be examined from time to time.

4.11.1 lsof

The lsof utility provides a list of all the currently open files on a system and indicates which Unix processes have opened them. lsof is available from ftp://vic.cc.purdue.edu/pub/tools/unix/lsof/.

4.11.2 ifstatus

The ifstatus utility monitors network connections for operation in debug or promiscuous mode which may indicate that information from a network connection is being given out to unauthorized parties. No output is produced by default from the application unless an alert situation is spotted, in which case the output can be configured to be sent via email to the system administrator. The ifstatus application is available from ftp://info.cert.org/pub/tools/ifstatus/.

4.12 Review

- First, be aware that there are various utilities installed with your operating system that can be used to determine information about networks and remote hosts. Develop the habit of using these tools, as well as the administrative tools that come with your operating system, in order to determine and maintain an awareness of normal usage patterns.
- Software tools that can search for vulnerabilities in your network are readily available from the Internet.
- Port scanners can be used to scan a host for listening ports, which indicate which services are likely to be running on the host.
- Network scanners scan a network comprehensively for weaknesses or vulnerabilities and give a report based on the scan results cross-referenced with a database of exploits.
- Denial of service applets exploit the use of 'illegal' network traffic that cause remote hosts to crash, disabling their network services. The best defence is to apply software patches.
- Back Orifice is an example of a more sophisticated client/server application which can be used to take control of a remote host that has been infected with the Back Orifice server. Most virus detection software detects infection by Back Orifice.
- Password crackers use a combination of dictionary cross-referencing and brute force guessing of words to crack passwords. They can be used offline if the password file of a computer has been obtained.
- Network analysers listen in to LAN traffic, and record traffic for subsequent analysis.
- File integrity and network monitoring tools can be used by the security or network administrator to further monitor usage.

4.13 To do

4.13.1 Gain familiarity with some tools of the trade

- On your laboratory system, download some of the tools discussed here and start to develop an appreciation of the way these tools could be used to scope out your network, and therefore where you can tighten up various aspects of your network's configuration.
- Start by installing a network server in your lab system that

reflects the typical set-up within your organization or of any your Internet facing servers.

- Use some of these tools and test them against this server. You should endeavour to use the following tools against your test server:
  1. Port scanner
  2. Network scanner
  3. Denial of service applets
- Telnet to the open ports, and note the banner messages or responses that are given off by the server applications. Find out how to configure the applications so that they remain anonymous instead. Remember, as soon as an application can be identified, vulnerabilities can be found against that application far easier than if the application is unknown.

5   Legal framework for network security

Ignorance of the law excuses no man; not that all men know the law, but because 'tis an excuse every man will plead, and no man can tell how to confute him.

(John Selden, English historian)

In 1995 Chevron was fined $2.2 million in a legal settlement with four female employees. The company was sued by the employees after an email containing '25 reasons why beer is better than women' was distributed on the company's network. The lesson to be learnt from this occurrence is clear! Allow employees uncontrolled use of network resources and your organization could end up in trouble, either through adverse publicity, or, worse still, through litigation and the ensuing consequences.

This chapter, therefore, discusses the legal use of computer networks, an aspect of network security often overlooked. As is often said, ignorance is no excuse in the eyes of the law, yet many organizations remain ignorant of their legal obligation with regard to the use of their computer networks. This is typified by the results of a survey reported in *Computer Weekly* magazine in mid-2001, which reported only 44 per cent of business websites surveyed complied with the basic requirements of the Data Protection Act 1998.

Lack of awareness of the relevant legal framework is unfortunate, as in many cases legislature makes a strong basis for an acceptable use policy within an organization. Compliance with legislature makes a rather more compelling case for an organization's acceptable use policy rather than the oft trotted out justification (excuses?) of 'wasting company time' or 'wasting resources'.

5.1 Which parts of the law are relevant to network security?

There is a perception that the law somehow does not apply to computers and, in particular, the Internet. This is untrue, although as far as network security is concerned there are only a few parliamentary Acts that can be thought of as being specific to computer networks and the Internet. The relevance of various Acts to network security is more usually defined through case law, which tests the application of various Acts of Parliament to novel situations not envisaged within the original scope of the Act. For instance, until judgment was passed on test cases, libel could not be said to occur on the Internet within the UK, and was an offence recognized only when committed in traditional printed media.

Establishing a useful legal framework for the use of the Internet through case law judgments has been protracted and sometimes difficult. Similar difficulties were encountered during the 1980s when attempts were made to establish case law against the growing problem of computer cracking. Then, an inability to adequately understand and define the problem of cracking meant that although there were clear incidences of wrongdoing, there was no means of prosecution open to the police. Only an Act of Parliament, the Computer Misuse Act 1990, was able to provide an adequate framework for protection against crackers, although there are many critics of the Act.

Crown territories

The UK legal system is complex, and is comprised of distinct legal systems of England, Northern Ireland, Scotland, and Wales. Each has a distinct judicial system of courts and legal professions. Outside of the UK legal system are those Crown territories that have not joined the United Kingdom and are therefore not subject to the United Kingdom's legal jurisdiction. Nevertheless, they remain part of the Crown and are known as Crown dependencies. Some have close business relations with the UK. There are three Crown dependants near the UK, each with their own legal systems related to but distinct from the UK legal system. These are the Isle of Man, a Crown dependency that has the longest legislature of any nation, over 800 years, and the Channel Islands which form two separate jurisdictions, that of Jersey, and that of Guernsey and the remaining islands. The main differences between the legislature of these Crown dependencies and that of the UK is the absence of data protection law, and also differences in financial and tax regulations. If you are working in a Crown dependency then you will need to check what impact the different legal system has on your organization's operation of computer networks. Much of what is applicable to in the UK will also apply to your own framework, though there may well be notable areas of differing practice.

Many of the pertinent Acts are reviewed below with examples of judgements that illustrate the application of the law to specific instances. Remember, we are interested in many of these cases not only because they show the potential for prosecution or punishment to third parties that commit wrongdoing against our organization but also so that we can become more aware of our own legal obligation. A pious sentiment but, nevertheless, one that will reduce the likelihood of litigation arising through the misuse of our networks. No matter how progressive or radical your organization, the law is rather less progressive and, whether right or wrong, is the benchmark against which our legal obligation is measured.

5.1.1 Libel and the Defamation Act 1996

Libel is a false publication that maliciously damages a person's reputation. Libel can also be interpreted as the act or instance of presenting such a statement to the public. On the Internet, where anyone can become an author, journalist, critic, and publisher, the potential for libel is huge. Libel on the Internet can be committed by posting Web pages, sending email, or by sending messages to bulletin boards on websites or Usenet, and the instantaneous nature of the medium means that many do not think prior to publication.

The main reason libel is committed on the Internet is the mistaken assumption that the Internet equates with 'free speech', an assumption that is certainly false in the UK. The ease with which libel can be committed, arguably, has also been facilitated by the deliberate hands-off policy from Internet Service Providers with regard to the content posted by their customers.

Free speech

The principle of free speech originates in the US Bill of Rights, an amendment to the Constitution of the United States of America drafted and ratified to provide protection to individual citizens from the actions of the state. The Bill of Rights was written in response to the alleged British violation of American civil rights, before and during the American Revolution. The first amendment reads: 'Congress shall make no law respecting an establishment of religion, or prohibiting the free exercise thereof; or abridging the freedom of speech, or of the press; or the right of the people peaceably to assemble, and to petition the Government for a redress of grievances.' Nevertheless, the extent to which speech can be made freely in the US must be seen in the context of limitations from other parts of the constitution and from law. These limitations are aimed particularly at obscenity, indecency, and with regard to minors. Certainly, the advent of the Internet is not the first time that new technology has precipitated a debate on free speech. The use of obscenities in television and the distribution of pornographic pictures when the camera was invented were both defended by appeal to the first amendment. The UK's Bill of Rights, by contrast, is altogether different and defines the prerogatives of the Crown rather than addressing the rights of individual citizens.

As is always the case when prosecuting a libel case, litigation can be costly and time consuming. Legal aid does not get awarded in instances of alleged libel. Then, there are additional challenges facing those who wish to tackle libel on the Internet, including the geographical cross-boundary nature of the Internet, the anonymity, and the transient nature of the material published.

But, case law has established a clear precedent for the applicability of the libel laws in the UK. What is emerging is that as far as the Act is concerned, the same rules apply to publication on the Internet as they do for any other printed medium. Two notable cases are reviewed below. One point to note is that

London is regarded as being the libel capital of the world. This point of view is held in part because of generous financial settlements, and the perceived weighting of libel laws in favour of the libelled. If your organization is accused of committing libel, you will probably pay the cost dearly.

Case Study – Defamation Act 1952: PC David Eggleton v. Asda (1995)

PC Eggleton was allegedly libelled by Asda following a complaint he had made. The complaint concerned some meat he had purchased from the shop and he had subsequently requested a refund for the meat. In response to PC Eggleton's complaint, an email containing the subject header 'Refund fraud – urgent, urgent, urgent' was distributed on Asda's internal email system, which suggested that the claim for refund was fraudulent. PC Eggleton discovered the message when he visited a local Asda branch to give advice about security. Printouts of the email were posted on noticeboards in the store, and a friend who worked there showed him the message.

Even though the email was only circulated within the organization, libel was deemed alleged to have been committed. The court found that as PC Eggleton was a policeman who dealt with the company, his character was called into question with the people with whom he was working. The case was settled before the trial concluded on terms that have not been publicly disclosed, and is notable because for the first time in the UK the law concerning libel had been tested with regard to email on a computer network.

Case Study – Defamation Act 1996: Western Provident Association (WPA) v. Norwich Union (1997)

During 1995, the Western Provident Association was alleged to be under investigation by the UK Department of Trade and Industry. Speculation mounted that the association was in general financial difficulties and would therefore be unable or unwilling to write any new policies. Norwich Union perpetuated this speculation by email within its organization; however, the email messages subsequently left Norwich Union and came to be in the possession of WPA. In the court case that followed, Norwich Union apologized to WPA and agreed to pay £450 000 damages plus costs for the defamatory email messages. To date, this remains the largest known libel settlement over a defamatory email. Again, this was only an internal email, but the case served as a clear warning to the UK business community that libel committed by email would be viewed by the courts very seriously indeed. Norwich Union suffered a great deal of adverse publicity as a result of this case.

5.1.2 Trade Description Act 1968, Consumer Protection Act 1987

Misrepresentation is where goods are advertised at a price that differs from the selling price. For instance, customers in a shop may be overcharged for goods when they reach the checkout, in comparison to the price stated on the label or shelf. The Trade Descriptions Act and the Consumer Protection Act oblige retailers to sell goods at the displayed price. There is no reason why these Acts should not be applied to ecommerce. Thus far, there have not been any relevant cases but some online retailers have been caught out. One incident concerned the catalogue retailer Argos who set up an ecommerce website. The website was suddenly swamped with online orders for a particular 21" Sony television. The reason for the sudden popularity of this product was that although the set should have been marked on the website as £299.99, the price was in fact marked as £3! One customer was reported to have asked for 1700 units and by the time Argos realized the mistake, orders had been taken for more than 300 000 televisions! Had this incident occurred in a normal shop, the retailer would have to sell at the marked price. But, after consultation with solicitors and the Advertising Standards Authority, Argos took the view that because no orders had been confirmed, no contract existed to sell the sets at £3.

5.1.3 Trade Marks Act 1994

The Trade Marks Act is notable because of the application of the Act to instances of cybersquatting. The term cybersquatting describes the 'unauthorized' registration of a company name or trademark, as a domain name, usually with the implicit aim of selling that domain name back to the larger company, or sometimes with some other way of benefiting from the registration in mind. Cybersquatting cases can be complicated by virtue of the fact that many of the attractive domain names are registered in the US, i.e. the generic top-level domain names. If there is a .com domain name involved, then the case may therefore have to be pursued in the US. One of the most famous cases is that of the company One in a Million, who registered variants of existing domain names of UK businesses. The company was later forced to hand over the names following legal proceedings. Another case, rather more complex, was that of Pitman Publishing and Pitman Training. The precedent seems to be clear, in that if your organization has registered trademarks, or has a history of using a name, this is clear grounds for retaining the use of that name on the Internet.

Case Study – Trade Marks Act 1994: Pitman Training Limited and PTC Oxford Ltd v. Nominet UK Ltd and Pearson Professional Ltd (1997)

This was a complex case, complicated by the fact that both parties had a historical association. Up until 1985, they were one and the same company. The companies parted and the dispute subsequently arose over the domain name pitman.co.uk and which company was entitled to use the name. The company was founded by Sir Issac Pitman in 1849, and consisted of a number of diverse divisions, including a publishing division, a training division and an examination division. These were sold off separately in 1985. Pitman Publishing was acquired by Pearsons, Pitman Training Ltd took the training business, and the examination business was taken over by a third party.

Pitman Training was permitted to use the Pitman name in connection with their business but only under specified conditions. In particular, they agreed not to use the name in connection with any business except that of its training and correspondence courses.

In February 1996 Pitman Publishing requested the registration of the domain name 'pitman.co.uk' for use in their publishing business. Receipt of the application was noted and confirmed on 21 February 1996.

In April 1996, however, Pitman Training made enquiries about the same domain name. On being told the domain name was available, Pitman Training duly registered the name and started to use the domain name in July of the same year.

Only until December 1996 was Pitman Publishing ready to go live with their email service and website. They found that not only had their domain name been reallocated to Pitman Training without their knowledge or consent, but also that Pitman Training had been using it already. Nominet therefore reallocated the domain name back to Pitman Publishing on 7

April 1997. Pitman Training immediately issued a writ seeking an injunction, which was granted ordering the name 'pitman.co.uk' be reassigned to Pitman Training pending a full hearing. There were three main grounds on which Pitman Training based their assertion that they were entitled to the domain name:

- Use by Pitman Publishing of the domain name 'pitman.co.uk' constituted passing off.
- Tortuous interference with contract.
- Abuse of process.

The application was refused on all three grounds. In fact, both Pitman Publishing and Pitman Training were equally entitled to use the name. Pitman Training, however, argued that passing off could be established due to their prior use of the domain name 'pitman.co.uk'. Just two email messages sent to Pitman Training were provided as evidence of this statement. Moreover, both companies had used the domain name in their respective advertisements. The court took the view that the only source of confusion arose from the fact that both businesses used the same name, and indeed were entitled to do so in their respective spheres of business. The court refused the application for the permanent injunction and ordered the reallocation of the domain name to Pitman Publishing. All else being equal, domain name registration is dealt with on a first come first served basis.

5.1.4 Obscene Publications Act 1959

Reports frequently appear in the news of organizations dismissing staff following the discovery of 'inappropriate material' being distributed on their networks. At NatWest Markets, staff were either sacked or formally disciplined following the circulation of pornography. This action was taken after the bank's Internet Service Provider noticed an increase in network traffic and alerted the bank. The increase in network traffic, due to the content being circulated, was so sudden that the network very quickly reached operational capacity!

A large number of staff at Barclays' stockbroking division were reportedly disciplined for similar offences, following allegations that illegal material was being circulated on the internal email system. According to reports, the only reason staff were not dismissed was that the numbers involved were so large, representing a sizeable proportion of employees in the office where the offences occurred. Several other high-profile cases are said to have occurred within many other companies.

But, in many instances companies misunderstand and distort the issues involved. On occasions, employees are chastized for displaying desktop wallpaper that in fact contains pictures far less revealing than those found in popular newspapers. On the other hand, those that have clearly broken the law are let off with a warning, and certainly without involvement of the police, lest the ensuing publicity cause damage to the company's reputation.

There is also a feeling that the law is not entirely clear as to what in facts constitutes pornographic material. According to the 1959 Act, obscenity is defined as follows:

> For the purposes of this Act an article shall be deemed to be obscene if its effect or (where the article comprises two or more distinct items) the effect of any one of its items is, if taken as a whole, such as to tend to deprave and corrupt persons who are likely, having regard to all relevant circumstances, to read, see or hear the matter contained or embodied in it.

So, for something to be deemed obscene, there is a need to show that persons will be depraved and corrupted; not easily demonstrated in practice. Recent amendments to the Act, contained in the Criminal Justice and Public Order Act 1994, have broadened the applicability of the Act to include the transmission of material electronically. Note also that the Telecommunications Act 1984 makes unlawful the transmission 'by means of a public telecommunications system, a message or other matter that is grossly offensive or of an indecent, obscene or menacing character'.

But, although there may be confusion as to what constitutes obscenity when the letter of the law is held up to scrutiny, the courts have shown no lack of clarity and vigour in pursuing obscenity cases. Common sense often dictates what is 'obsence' and what therefore should not be transmitted or stored on your networks. The subject of inappropriate content and content control is returned to in later chapters.

5.1.5 Copyright Designs and Patents Act 1988

The nature of copyright is often misunderstood, but is easy to grasp. Copyright exists in the way that knowledge or material is presented. No copyright is held over the actual knowledge or material. For instance, this book is subject to copyright, but the knowledge contained within is not subject to copyright controls.

One consequence of the widespread availability of information on the Internet is the ease with which information may be accessed and then copied for use elsewhere. The most prevalent instance of copyright breach is through the use of images that have been taken from one website and then placed onto another website without the copyright owner's permission. Several businesses that rely on the value and originality of their website images, such as dealers in stock photography, or dealers in other types of photography, are said to employ 'copyright detectives' to search the Web for possible breaches, if a breach has indeed occurred, then action is taken. There are several reported instances concerning unofficial 'fan-sites' devoted to various pop groups or singers that have been closed by recording companies.

Determining whether breaches have occurred through misuse of text content is somewhat more difficult to determine. There are several ways in which textual copyright breaches might occur.

- 'Cutting and pasting' content from one sight to another.
- Linking from one site to another.
- Framing one site within another site using the <FRAMES> HTML tag.

There have been some notable cases recently where the application of copyright law to the Internet has been tested, but to avoid litigation the best rule of thumb is to ask the copyright owner's permission first before including any material from their website or any other Internet source. In many cases, the copyright owner is only too happy to let the material be reused, sometimes with only the smallest of credit being given. Sometimes, though, a cavalier approach to copyright leads to trouble.

Case Study – Copyright Design and Patents Act 1988: Countrywide Assured v. Homemovers

Countrywide Assured and Homemovers are both estate agents that use the Web as a means of advertising properties for sale. The companies own, respectively, the website addresses www.right-move.co.uk and www.homemovers.co.uk. Countrywide Assured accused Homemovers of copying details concerning properties from their database on the rightmove.co.uk website, without consent being given. The writ issued by Countrywide Assured included a claim that the copyright infringement warranted damages payable under the Copyright Designs and Patents Act. When the case came to court, Homemovers conceded and settled, agreeing not to use information from Countrywide Assured in future. The grounds for litigation are thought to have arisen from the Copyright and Rights in Databases Regulations introduced in January 1997. The case is interesting because this was the first time that these new regulations had been tested. The regulations provide copyright protection for databases in which there has been substantial investment. This case should serve to further clarify the way in which UK law can protect information held and distributed on the Internet.

5.1.6 Data Protection Act 1998

Within the UK, the use of all data records regarding personal information is governed by the Data Protection Act 1998. This Act lays down strict procedures which data controllers and users must adhere to. The 1998 Act was tabled in Parliament to address the implications of imminent legalisation from the EU concerning an individual's right to privacy, and superseded the 1984 Data Protection Act which detailed the extent to which organizations may hold and process information gathered and held about private individuals. The EU Data Protection Directive from which the 1998 Act is derived requires 'Member States to protect the fundamental rights and freedoms of natural persons, in particular their right to privacy with respect to the processing of personal data'. This principle is included within the 1998 Act.

Even of late, many businesses remain unaware of the implications of the new Act, which became law on 1 March 2000, and some remain completely unaware of the Act altogether. The consequences of non-compliance are serious. An organization found guilty of offences under the Data Protection Act could be liable to an unlimited fine. Directors can also be held personally liable if the company can be shown to have acted with their knowledge or if the offence was committed due to their negligence.

The main points concerning the new Act are summarized below.

- The 1998 Act restates the eight data protection principles, that data must be:
  1. Fairly and lawfully processed
  2. Processed for limited purposes
  3. Adequate, relevant and not excessive
  4. Accurate
  5. Not kept longer than necessary
  6. Processed in accordance with the data subject's rights
  7. Secure
  8. Not transferred to countries without adequate protection
- Data protection is extended to certain manual records as well as to computerized personal data.
- Conditions are introduced, which must be satisfied, if personal data is to be processed, with additional conditions to be met for sensitive data such as data about an individual's ethnic origin, health, or sex life.
- The rights of individuals are defined, for instance organizations must divulge to individuals who is processing personal data about them and for what reason.
- Individuals have the right to prevent personal data being used for direct marketing.
- There are rules for the transfer of personal data beyond the perimeter of the European Union.

Any organization must be able to deal formally with requests for access to personal data within specified time limits. A request for information must be made in writing, but the Act is clear that the request may be made by electronic means such as email. Companies and organizations that wish to process personal data must nominate themselves, as data controllers, to the Data Protection Registrar. The Registrar will hold an entry against each data controller that includes the name and address of the data controller and a general description of the processing of personal data by a data controller.

Despite the lack of data protection laws in the US, there is growing concern about the extent to which personal privacy can be relegated in the quest for consumer information by businesses. There are hundreds of bills being considered within the various states, and there is a growing pressure for federal bills. Two incidents in particular have underlined the lack of protection for consumers.

First, there was the collapse of the ecommerce site Toysmart.com, which attempted to sell their database of consumer information accumulated, after reassuring users that their personal data would not be sold to any third party. The database was later destroyed following a legal wrangle with the Federal Trade Commission. Then, perhaps more widely reported, there was the instance when online marketing company DoubleClick wanted to merge a database of consumers' online preferences the company managed with another database, acquired through a company takeover, that held consumer preferences and details taken from mail order business. This would enable consumers' online preferences to be cross-referenced with their names, addresses, etc. Again, the Federal Trade Commission intervened.

There have been relatively few prosecutions under the Data Protection Act, but one notable case was that of the Crown v. US Robotics under the earlier Act. US Robotics, now known as 3COM, were fined the rather small sum of £2730 for breach of the Data Protection Act 1984. This was for holding customer and reseller information collected from the company website on company databases, without registering this activity with the Data Protection Registrar.

5.1.7 Computer Misuse Act 1990

The Computer Misuse Act 1990 was passed through Parliament following heightened concern at the time of the increasing incidence of computer cracking, i.e. the unauthorized access to third party computer systems, and the apparent inability of existing legislation to tackle the problem adequately. Prior to the introduction of this Act, several prosecutions against crackers had failed. These were made on the basis of existing Acts, usually drawing on the premise that data had been stolen.

Offences committed against the Computer Misuse Act are punishable by imprisonment, and the Act covers three specific areas:

- Unauthorized access to computer material – actions carried out in breach of this particular section need not be carried out against any particular system or data.
- Unauthorized access with intent to commit or facilitate commission of further offences.
- Unauthorized modification of computer material – this is the part of the Act that covers the damage done to computers through viruses.

Such security breaches can occur quite simply, perhaps through poor password control on information systems. Any user can then take advantage of poor controls to browse computer files that they should not be privy to. More concerted efforts to crack a computer system can be made with the help of software tools such as those provided by organizations like the Cult of the Dead Cow, e.g. Back Orifice, which exploit known weaknesses in operating systems. According to the Computer Misuse Act, downloading and possessing these applications is not illegal. The Act is very clear, though – to utilize these tools and attempt to break into another system is illegal. This means that merely being in possession of cracking tools should not be grounds for police involvement.

One of the early prosecutions under the Act was that against Datastream Cowboy and Kuji. These two crackers were alleged to have broken into the US Department of Defense network. Because they were resident in the UK, they were beyond the jurisdiction of the US. They were not off the hook, however, and were charged with having committed acts that were in breach of the Computer Misuse Act 1990, under sections 1 and 3.

The Act also offers legal recourse against the authors of computer viruses. The author of the virus SMEG, Christopher Pile, was caught out, prosecuted successfully and sentenced to 18 months under sections 2 and 3 of the Computer Misuse Act.

Industry commentators have also suggested a more novel application of the Computer Misuse Act in order to deal with the problem of unsolicited email. In the early days of corporate Internet use, unsolicited email became a growing problem, compounded by the fact that early Web browser clients were often made to be able to divulge email addresses. IT users saw no way of redress. As the Computer Misuse Act legislates against the unauthorized modification of computer material, some saw this as providing some protection against junk mail. Each email received by a user is stored on the local system, either locally on that user's hard drive, or on the user's office server. Literally speaking, the receipt of an unsolicited email will modify the hard drive where the email is stored. This point was not tested in court, though, as EU data protection directives appeared at the time to offer a more robust solution.

5.1.8 Electronic Communications Act 2000

The main aim of the Electronic Communications Act is to provide confidence in ecommerce and peripheral technology. The Act provides the legal framework for this by providing:

- An approvals scheme for businesses and other organizations providing cryptography services, including electronic signature and confidentiality services.
- The legal recognition of electronic signatures and their verification.
- The removal of obstacles in other legislation to the use of electronic communication and storage in place of paper.

The motive for the Act was mainly the desire of the Government to make the UK a place where ecommerce can flourish. This should be seen in the context of deadlines set by the UK Government for all government services to be deliverable on the Internet before 2005.

The Act is in two main parts:

- The first part relates to cryptography service providers and concerns the arrangements for registering providers of cryptography support services, such as electronic signature services and confidentiality services.
- The second part is aimed at the facilitation of electronic commerce, data storage, etc. This makes provision for the legal recognition of electronic signatures and the process under which they may be generated, communicated or verified. It also facilitates the use of electronic communications or electronic storage of information, as an alternative to traditional means of communication or storage.

A consequence of the Act is that the Secretary of State will establish and maintain a register of approved providers of cryptography support services. The public will be able to have access to the register and any changes to the register will be publicized. The main aim of the register is to provide a ready reference to the public of organizations that have been assessed against various quality criteria, in order that use of their services will be encouraged. The register will be voluntary, though one presumes that inclusion might be a requirement in order to participate in government ecommerce procurement.

5.1.9 Regulation of Investigatory Powers Act 2000

The Regulation of Investigatory Powers Bill was brought before the House of Commons on 9 February 2000 and received Royal Assent on 28 July 2000. With regard to this Act, one thing is certain, few pieces of parliamentary legislature have caused such a debate within the IT and wider business community.

The aim of the Act is to include within government legislation reference to contemporary technologies in order to tap and eavesdrop legally into suspected criminal activity. The main technology in mind is the Internet, and the Regulation of Investigating Powers Act was welcomed by many in the area of law enforcement due to the fact that the Interception of Communications Act 1985 did not provide adequate provision for intercepting communication by the Internet. Encrypted email, for instance, could not be legally intercepted and decrypted.

There are four main areas within the Act's scope:

- Interception of communications.
- Surveillance and covert human intelligence sources.
- Investigation of electronic encrypted data.
- Scrutiny of investigatory powers and the functions of the intelligence services.

Most of the criticism of the Act has been directed at the obligations that could be placed on businesses that provide or utilize Internet connectivity. Clause 49 of the Act states that with the 'appropriate permission', a third party who has, or has had, a decryption key, shall be obliged to provide either the key or instead plain text of specified material. Failure to comply with this proposed action could mean imprisonment and/or an unlimited fine.

In all likelihood, in order that organizations can comply with the requirements of the Act, a substantial management overhead will be incurred due to the need for encryption key management, tracking and recording copies of the email and other transactions that an organization sends. In order to recompense any company that is instructed to hand over a key or message, the Government is proposing a compensation mechanism for affected firms.

But, perhaps one of the most objectionable parts of the Bill is the implicit presumption of guilt in the instance of a key owner losing the said key. Should this issue arise, the person who has allegedly lost the key will have to prove this point in court, i.e. innocence will have to be demonstrated. Note that the Bill is aimed squarely at providing Government with extended powers. The Bill is not aimed at providing any powers to business to intercept or otherwise monitor communications for the purposes of quality control, training, or the like.

Case Study – The principality of Sealand and the Regulation of Investigatory Powers Act

Sealand is a fortress 12 miles off the coast of Felixstowe, and is a self-proclaimed principality claiming to be beyond the jurisdiction of the UK. The claim is based on the fact that territorial waters of the UK extend for just 5 miles from the shore, hence Sealand is apparently well beyond the UK's judicial reach. To take advantage of this situation, a company called HavenCo, registered in Anguilla, was set up and is being promoted as an offshore data storage company. Due to Sealand's location, HavenCo is able to operate as a data storage provider that is beyond the reach of the Regulation of Investigatory Powers Act.

Under the Act, encryption keys are required to be divulged to the police or security services on demand, even if this breaches confidentiality agreements that may have been signed by the parties involved. Moreover, this requirement for divulgence requires organizations to put in place procedures to make encryption keys and details of transactions available at short notice. This is seen as contrary to the interests of many organizations and their customers, and HavenCo could provide a viable alternative proposition to many organizations that would rather avoid the perceived conflict of interest and obligations that the Act imposes.

5.2 Review

- Although the common perception is that computer systems and the Internet are largely unregulated under UK law, this is not the case. There is an increasing body of case law, with reference to existing parliamentary Acts, that provides guidance regarding what can and cannot be done.
- In addition to case law judgments, there are several Acts of Parliament that have been passed specifically to moderate appropriate use of computer networks, and the way that data is handled and stored on those networks.
- You should be particularly aware of the following Acts of Parliament, which have either been used successfully in prosecuting offences conducted in the Internet, or which pertain to computer network use.
  1. Defamation Act 1996.
  2. Trade Description Act 1968.
  3. Consumer Protection Act 1987.
  4. Trade Marks Act 1994.

5. Obscene Publications Act 1959.
6. Copyright Designs and Patents Act 1988.
7. Data Protection Act 1998.
8. Computer Misuse Act 1990.
9. Electronics Communications Act 2000.
10. Regulation of Investigatory Powers Act 2000.

5.3 To do

5.3.1 Establish your legal position

- Speak to your organization's legal department and bring these various Acts to their attention in order to establish your position clearly. If you have no legal department, then speak to your solicitor, local Chamber of Commerce, professional association, or some similar organization.

- Monitor closely the position regarding employees' right to privacy in the workplace, with regard to monitoring email and other forms of communication. This is one area of the law that appears to be in a state of flux, and may be influenced by the Human Rights Act.

- Start to educate employees about the very real legal implications of using the Internet. The biggest danger for many organizations is with regard to email. Disclaimers *might* help to distance your organization from statements expressed by email, though they will not allow you to absolve responsibility completely.

- The Data Protection Act 1998 appears to have caught many organizations off guard. Speak to your organization's sales and marketing department and establish a shared basic understanding of your organization's obligations under this new Act. Pay attention to the way information is stored and used. Look at your organization's website and establish whether any caveats or permissions should be sought where personal information is gathered from the website. This applies to any organization that is gathering data within the EU, and special rules apply if that data is to be exported from the EU.

- Together with your legal department, or similar, draw up a strategy of legal compliance and communicate this to employees in readiness for inclusion within the security policy.

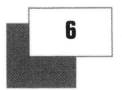

6 Gaining intelligence and taking action

Fine words butter no parsnips.
(Seventeenth century English proverb, with the same sentiment
as the more recent 'Actions speak louder than words')

6.1 Introduction

If you have read the previous chapters of this book you should
now be well aware of the threats to network security, and of the
cost of security breaches. You are convinced of the seriousness
of the problem, and what you are looking for now is a plan of
action whereby you can make your own network more secure.
What is needed is a plan of action to:

- Baseline your understanding of the security problem domain.
- Update your operating system by applying all the service
  packs, patches or hot fixes that are required.
- Conduct a risk assessment to establish the threats to your
  network security that are likely to arise.
- Make any configuration changes that are required. Secure
  configuration is discussed in the following chapter.
- Ensure you are taking data backups and are ready to restore
  that data in the event of disaster recovery being required.
- Define a policy for acceptable use within the workplace applicable to all network users.
- Assess the requirement for, and then implement, technical
  solutions such as firewalls and content security.
- Document and publish your network security policy

describing the implementation and management of all the above measures.

The remainder of the book tackles these areas of network security in turn, and this order of presentation reflects an order of priority that should be given to securing a network on the basis of the likelihood of various risks arising. Policy documentation is presented in the final chapter, as in order to tackle policy, some understanding of the threats and measures implemented within your organization is needed.

So, to start with, in this chapter we consider the steps that can be taken in order to gain intelligence and commence action in the management of your network security. There are two steps to this: first, the development of your own awareness, and second, the precipitation of your organization's awareness of network security in readiness for the work that needs to be done in establishing and implementing a network security policy. Let's start, though, with a surprisingly simple suggestion – go and surf the Web! The Web contains a massive amount of information concerning network security, not only to be found on vendor specific websites relevant to your operating systems and software, but also in general network security websites that are not vendor specific.

6.1.1 Vendor websites

Vendor websites contain operating system specific information regarding known vulnerabilities, holes, and also contain patches, service packs and hot fixes that can be applied to your software. Look for your operating system, and also for the large software applications you use, such as office productivity suites or back office server applications.

Linux

http://www.linux.org/
contains a section which has all the HOWTO documents listed. There is a security-HOWTO document for the various Linux distributions that are now available. Also, there is a website specifically for Linux security, called www.linuxsecurity.com.

Microsoft

http://www.microsoft.com/security
contains links to articles on some of the security issues pertinent

to the Microsoft Windows operating system family. Service packs and hot fixes should be listed here, or you could look in the relevant section for each specific Windows version.

Sun Microsystems

http://www.sun.com/security
provides a first port of call for Solaris and SunOS system administrators.

6.1.2 Non vendor websites

There are countless security websites that are not tied in to specific vendors, and are instead written by and contributed to industry commentators and experts. Some of these non-vendor websites are also good sources of information.

http://www.ntsecurity.com
is a good first stop in the search for an alternative version of Windows security issues. This site does not pull punches and contains a wide range of resources. Try also:
http://www.ntbugtraq.com
http://www.securitywatch.com

http://www.cert.org
is a canonical source of security issues, though some may find the site to be Unix centric. Don't let the emphasis on Unix put you off, though, the advice is sound.

http://www.alw.nih.gov/Security/security.html
is a good portal site for a variety of resources.

http://www.ciac.org/ciac/
is another good information source.

http://www.atstake.com/research/index.html
includes information about the l0pht crack tool used for cracking Windows NT passwords. NB the 0 in l0pht is a zero, not a capital O.

http://www.codc.com
is the home of the Cult of the Dead Cow, developers of the Back Orifice client and server.

http://www.hackersclub.com
is another typical crackers forum. Have a look at the archives of websites that have been cracked.

6.2 Usenet news groups

When you have finished surfing the Web, there is another resource that you should consider using, the Usenet news groups. These are sometimes available on your corporate network, and there are several Usenet news groups dedicated to security. If you are not able to find Usenet news on your business network, then you may be able to locate them through your ISP, or you can access news groups through various websites, such as http://groups.google.com.

Some of these groups, by virtue of being unregulated, can be rather anarchic in their content. Also, when posting queries to these newsgroups, particularly if you are new to security, circa 50 per cent of the responses are likely to be useless. But, if you sort the wheat from the chaff, then you can elicit some useful responses. A word of warning: do not give away too much information when posting queries. If you are discussing vulnerabilities or weaknesses in your network, then discuss the problem in general terms, and certainly avoid divulging IP addresses and account details. Some of the news groups are listed below. A '*' in the listing acts as a wildcard and indicates that there are several groups within the main heading provided.

comp.security.*
contains groups that include discussion of Unix security issues, such as comp.security.unix, groups that discuss firewalls, such as comp.security.firewalls, and security announcements, such as comp.security.announce.

comp.os.*
contains various groups related to various operating systems. There is a discussion of NT security issues in comp.os.ms-windows.nt.admin.security, for instance.

alt.computer.*
contains unmoderated newsgroups, including alt.computer. security which is concerned with security issues about all operating systems.

alt.crackers
contains discussion of security issues from an alternative perspective.

6.3 Specialist press

The specialist computer press can be a valuable source of information and often contains digest or review articles that have a wider perspective of security issues and their effect on the management of information systems. There are a plethora of free computer magazines which, as a manager or IT professional, you most likely qualify to receive copies through the post free of charge. Make sure that you are on the subscription list for:

Computer Weekly
Subscribe at http://www.cw365.com. The *Computer Weekly* website has a security forum, and a search facility that enables users to search through previously published editorial and news content.

Computing
Subscribe at http://www.computingnet.co.uk.

Network Week
Subscribe at http://www.techweb.com.

PC Week
Subscribe at http://www.pcweek.co.uk.

IT Week
Subscribe at http://www.zdnet.co.uk/itweek.

6.4 Events and seminars

Of course, as soon as you subscribe to these magazines you will probably get several invitations through the post for seminars, exhibitions and other events. Although in some way these tend to be sales pitches, they can nevertheless provide a good opportunity to hear the experts and see their software and hardware first hand. One-day seminars are frequently held by security product vendors and these can be an excellent way of getting a background and feel for security issues. A drawback of these seminars is that the solutions offered by vendors are biased and are sometimes therefore overly prescriptive toward technical solutions. Dates and venues for these events are printed in the publications listed above; in addition you may find details of events in vendors' websites. I recall going to a particularly good event held by Network Associates, where the speakers were confident enough to give a live demonstration of their software, not just simulated displays or screen shots!

But, if you work for a particularly large organization, then there is no reason why a seminar could not be held in-house. You could invite all interested parties to a half-day or one-day seminar where you could give a keynote presentation and you could then invite vendors to come and speak. Most vendors will send along a member of their sales team, just as long as you can guarantee an audience with a budget. This would certainly raise the profile of security in your organization. If you belong to a smaller organization, why not arrange an event through your Chamber of Commerce, or some other local professional body?

6.5 Books

There is a great deal of choice when buying books about computer security. Unfortunately there are three drawbacks to buying such books: first, many concentrate on Unix at the expense of Microsoft Windows, second, by default, they can appear rather dated fairly quickly, and third, they can at times be rather too technical and in-depth for the non-specialist to grasp. The best plan is to check the publication date before you buy and to have a thorough look at the table of contents.

One of the best buying resources for books is amazon.co.uk. This website contains a massive choice of books. The site can be searched by category or keyword, but be sure to use more than just 'security' otherwise you will be deluged with results! One book I would recommend is *Practical Unix and Internet Security* by Simson Garfinkel and Gene Spafford, published by O'Reilly.

6.6 Taking action

Right, now that you have immersed yourself into security issues, read your manuals, visited the websites, been to seminars and conferences, you probably feel ready to take action. A word of warning: do not take a knee-jerk response. Instead think through carefully about how you can address the security issues you are faced with. The temptation is to apply simple measures, like denying access to the Web, for example, so that exposure to threats is eliminated rather than managed. The trade-off from such a simplistic approach is that your organization will be denied all the benefits of the Web at the same time as being immune from the threats.

The remainder of this book is focused in the main on helping you to address your network security with a measured approach. But, prior to taking any of these actions you should first carry out a preliminary assessment of your hardware and software platforms. The remainder of this chapter deals with this matter. Also, do not forget to complete the incident book, discussed in Chapter 3's 'To do' (p. 54).

6.6.1 Carry out an inventory

Although you may feel you know your network system well, you might still be surprised about just how much legacy, or unknown, hardware and software is still being utilized. Moreover, there might be some more modern hardware about that is compromising all your existing security measures, such as an external USB modem that is plugged into a computer on your secure network, and therefore enabling one or more users to bypass all your expensive firewalls.

Do not assume anything. Walk about and investigate what you have deployed. You need to identify and take note of important information concerning each computer. Be as detailed as possible, for instance when dealing with network cards you will need to know the make, type, release, address, capacity, and will need to ensure that you have the latest version of the network driver to hand. Use the Internet to locate the latest versions of all your drivers. In addition to taking the computer inventory, you should include other network equipment, such as printers, hubs, routers, etc., and assets such as software installation disks, manuals, and data recovery media. A template is provided at the end of this chapter. Paper copies of the inventory should be kept, as well as master soft copies, as paper copies are a bit more portable and are useful in the event of a crisis such as computer failure.

6.6.2 Patch your software

When you have a clear idea about the operating system including the major and minor release numbers, and the software including the major and minor release numbers, you should then visit the appropriate vendor website and establish whether or not you are using the latest releases. This is important, because bugs and holes are being discovered in commonly used software frequently, and these are then updated by the software vendors and posted for general use on the vendors' websites.

Windows

Microsoft software updates are called service packs. You can establish the version of the Windows you are using, i.e. the service pack number, during the initial bootup. These service packs are posted on the relevant Windows family section of the Microsoft website and are available to download. Service packs are quite sizeable so you may wish to copy the service pack onto a CD or place on the Intranet for use by others in your company, to save bandwidth and time.

Service packs are easy to install, all you need to do is to log into the administrator account, and then execute the installation program. The rest of the installation is automated. The only note of caution should be that if you later install other parts of the Windows file system from your CD, you should then reinstall the service pack to ensure that the latest service pack files are used.

Some versions of Windows also contain the option of conducting a Windows update online. This can be a useful way of establishing which parts of your installation require updating, but you might wish to conduct some of the legwork yourself by visiting the website and manually browsing.

In addition to service packs, Microsoft often release hot fixes that are smaller more specific updates, sometimes referred to as patches in the Unix world. These are for specific software applications and are considerably smaller than service packs. Installation of hot fixes is usually self-explanatory. They are downloaded and then executed, and are accompanied by instructions.

Unix

The speed with which updates are available for Unix systems is generally much faster than for Windows. On at least one occasion, patches for major bugs have been released less than one hour after a bug was first reported on the Internet.

There are two ways you can patch software with Unix systems. First, you can either patch individual software applications, such as the mail package or the Web server, by installing single patch files on the file system. These are usually available on the software developer's website, which may or may not be the same as the software vendor.

The alternative is to install the next minor version of the software operating system. Unix systems tend to be released with a great deal more frequency than their Windows counterpart. In particular, Linux kernels are released on virtually a weekly basis. Note that there is always the temptation to get caught in an upgrade trap. If you are using a fairly recent release, use patches instead of complete upgrades. Remember: if it ain't broke don't fix it. Only install patches in response to security vulnerabilities.

6.6.3 Stay on the ball

In carrying out the above actions, taking an inventory and then patching the software, you have effectively baselined your operating system and software. You are now in a position to start to manage your system's security in a pre-emptive fashion rather than just react to security incidents as they happen. There are two key facets to managing your system's security.

- First, you must stay informed about new threats as they emerge.
- Second, you must draft and implement policy for using the systems in a secure fashion, for the benefit of administrators and users alike.

The best way to stay informed is to keep visiting the forum you have identified as being suited for your operating system. You are better off using the Internet as your primary information source rather than printed material, if for no other reason than the fact that there is always a period of latency involved while the stories are being written and the paper printed.

One way of ensuring that you stay informed is to subscribe to one of the many email lists. Subscription to a list will ensure that you receive any news in a timely fashion and removes the impetus from you to keep looking at the same website time after time. These lists should not be confused with commercial mailing lists, you should not be inundated with spam as a result of subscribing to any of the mainstream security mailing lists, in particular the CERT list.

6.7 Review

- Participate in security forums. Go to the vendor shows and seminars, and if you work in a large organization, then organize an event in-house.
- Take stock of your network infrastructure and keep the information to hand. A template is provided at the end of this chapter.

- When you have established through the inventory taking what operating systems and software you have, you need to check the vendor's website and see what updates are available. Then, install the latest patches and service packs for your system.
- Finally, having baselined your network's software, stay on the ball. Be ready to act in the case of new alerts.

6.8 To do

6.8.1 Take action

- Browse the security websites, pick one that you like the look of and make a habit of visiting the site once a day for a few minutes at a time. Register with an email bulletin list from another site you like the look of.
- Conduct the inventory using the template herein as a start point, adding your own data fields as necessary.
- Download and install the latest patches and service packs. Remember then to update the inventory accordingly.
- Start to think now about the further steps you can take to add to the security of your network, such as establishing disaster recovery plans, policy for acceptable use, and the deployment of technical measures. These are discussed in later chapters.
- If you haven't already done so, start to complete the incident book as discussed in Chapter 3's 'To do'.

6.9 Computer inventory template

Asset Number
Asset Type
Server   Workstation   Router   Hub   Switch   Bridge
Other:
Manufacturer
Model
Serial number
Vendor

Asset location
Asset owner
Installed by:
Maintained by:

Operating system   Version   Mandatory service packs/patches

IP addressing scheme
IP address:
Subnet mask:
Gateway:
DNS:
WINS:
Static routes:

Main board type
Processor
RAM capacity

Storage	**Manufacturer**	**Model**	**Capacity**
Hard drives			
Floppy drives			
CD-ROM			
Removable media			
SCSI controller			

Peripherals	**Manufacturer**	**Model**
Video card		
Sound card		
Network card		
Modem		
ISDN TA		
Other		

Application software	**Version**	**Mandatory service packs/patches**

7

Secure processes and system configuration

Microsoft® Windows NT® operating system provides a rich set of
security features. However, the default out-of-the-box configuration is
highly relaxed, especially on the Workstation product. This is because
the operating system is sold as a shrink-wrapped product with an
assumption that an average customer may not want to worry about
a highly restrained but secure system on their desktop.
(Securing Windows NT 4.0 Installation,
11 August 1997, from www.microsoft.com)

7.1 Introduction

After the baselining activities outlined in Chapter 6, the next
stage in your security programme is to improve on the secure
configuration of your network. First, we shall start with physical security, one of the most often overlooked aspects to
securing the network and one that is easy to remedy.

7.2 Physical security

Physical security addresses the environment in which the
server and the client computers are located, accessed and
used. The server needs to be situated somewhere out of the
way, so that there is no possibility of interference by anyone.
Certainly you would not want the cleaners dusting the
computer cases or pulling out the server's power supply for
their vacuum cleaners. How many situations have you
encountered where the secure server is kept in the most

insecure of settings? There are instances where servers have been located in open offices next to the coffee machine, for instance, or next to public access Internet computers. But, the most bizarre and surreal location for a network server I have seen was that of the server located within a spare cubicle, inside the ladies' toilets! The same company also managed to install a racking system within such a confined space, that the equipment overheated. The air conditioning unit that was subsequently installed to counter the problem was then mounted so close to the rack that the rack door was unable to be opened fully!

As well as servers, the desktop workstations also need a degree of protection. The protection applied to your workstations should of course be related to their value as capital assets, and also in terms of their ability to be used to access your data. Finally, what about the protection offered to all the cabling and peripherals that are used, including the manner in which the cables are routed around the workplace? Some of these aspects of physical security are discussed below.

7.2.1 The operational environment

The first item to address when considering physical security is the operational environment of the organization. Whether or not your building or premises are secure will, to a large extent, dictate the degree of protection that you can offer to individual pieces of the your network hardware. Being simplistic, installing all the firewalls in the world would be rather pointless if someone could just walk into your office and steal a laptop or a desktop computer. Worse still, what about if someone could gain easy access to information held on the server by connecting to the network? There are many reported incidents of unauthorized individuals with electronic equipment gaining access inside businesses or government organizations and being left to their own devices for hours, often masquerading as maintenance staff.

Many organizations choose to use the following protection measures in order to secure their operational environment:

- Control of access to the building, by use of limited entry points and staffed reception areas, where guests are required to sign in.
- Use of identity badges in order to distinguish between guests and staff, and sometimes to differentiate between varying levels of access for staff.

- Use of swipe card, keypad, or other means of ensuring access throughout the building is controlled.
- Care and attention is given to the appropriate closure of windows, fire doors, and other unmanned access points.
- Equipment being used for sensitive work is protected with an adequate level of additional security if required.
- Network servers are protected with an adequate level of protection to prevent casual access.

The physical location of the hardware should be commensurate with the level of security and availability required. Usually the server will be isolated and accessed directly by just a few individuals. In contrast, the type of protection afforded to workstations is likely to be different to servers, due to their location within a more open working environment. These days many staff are situated in open plan offices where access is often unrestricted. Physical security of workstation clients is seen by many organizations as not being as critical as that of servers, and to an extent there is some truth in that premise. Damage to the computer workstation, or even theft, while an unfortunate occurrence, would most likely not be such a big issue as computers are increasingly becoming commodity items to larger businesses, and are readily replaceable. This is particularly true if the desktop computer is used simply as a bare client in order to gain access to the server, and has no data storage facility locally, such as hard drives, or the like.

In some cases, however, desktop computers are equipped with hard drives and will therefore have data stored locally, whether in the form of temporary files or in the form of users' files, instead of on the server. The protection afforded to servers and workstations therefore needs to be provided after careful consideration of the value of the data stored on the computer if that computer were stolen. The following points should be considered.

7.2.2 Servers

- Location: Servers should be kept in a locked and secure room, which is purpose allocated. Some advocate the use of glass doors or walls so that any unauthorized activity can be observed.
- Access: Should be controlled to specified individuals who have a need to physically access the servers.
- Air conditioning: The room should be air conditioned in order that the optimal operating temperature of the servers is maintained.

- Air humidity: Some computers will function with increased fault tolerance if humidity levels can be maintained at optimum levels.
- Power supply: Of course, servers should be provided with a UPS.

7.2.3 Workstations

- Security marking: this can be hidden from everyday view, but nevertheless is large enough to be a deterrent to a thief. Monitors can be marked on their backs or undersides. Base units can be marked on the backs, or in the case of the flat desktop cases, on the part of the case where the monitor sits. Marking serves as a deterrent, providing any thief with the hassle of having to remove the marking prior to disposal in most instances. Security stickers are available which are nigh on impossible to peel off cleanly, or, as an alternative, security marker pens can be used.
- Steel cables: these can be used to tie down base units and monitors, but these are unsightly and sometimes offer little protection, apart from protection against the casual or opportunist thief. They may have a use with laptops, though, and can be carried around with the laptop computer.
- Full inventory: this should be taken and maintained regularly so that instances of unauthorized movement of equipment can be noted and investigated.
- Computer cases: these should be fastened with security screws that are unable to be opened with a normal Phillips or flat head screwdriver. Alternatively, consider some other means of locking the case shut in order to prevent theft or removal of computer memory or other peripheral cards. This also prevents the unauthorized installation of hardware, such as TV tuner cards, and also enables the computer to be protected from tampering.

7.2.4 Printers

Like computer workstations, computer printers are portable and are susceptible to theft or unauthorized removal. Printers need to be secured to their area of deployment, and it may be easier to physically tie down a printer than a workstation. You can also employ security marking on most printer cases to good effect.

7.2.5 Hubs, bridges and routers

Hubs, bridges and routers need to be afforded careful protection, with a degree of security more akin to servers than to workstations. Many organizations keep their network hardware in rooms similar to those where their servers are located. Network hardware should not be tampered with, the removal of a cable by accident or otherwise could bring an entire office network to a halt and would be difficult to isolate quickly.

- Keep routers in a secure, locked area if possible.
- Even better, house routers in a purpose-built cabinet.
- Ensure that cables are securely installed into the router; if possible tag each cable with the network address you are using, unless of course you are using a dynamic host addressing scheme such as DHCP.

7.2.6 Cabling

Cables, and for this purpose fibre optical connections, are almost always used to connect together various components of a network, such as clients to servers, and into hubs, bridges and routers, and other associated network hardware. Cables cost very little, but are crucial to the operation of a network. Yet, perhaps because they are so cheap, their physical security is often overlooked.

Many offices suffer from cables being draped over furniture or allowed to lie across the floor unprotected. I have seen one instance of cables looped out of exterior windows between offices, in what was a high security environment! In such circumstances, before long a cable will become snagged free from the wall socket or from the network card, or may be broken. In the case of the more modern 10 base T or 100 base T cable this would be a localized problem affecting perhaps just one computer. But in the case of the older BNC/COAX cable, just one snagged cable or broken connection will most likely bring a part of the network down, as a circuit must be complete in order for the network to function. Locating a cable that has worked lose, or that has broken, is time consuming to say the least. Just a small office with ten or 20 users might spend a few hours looking for the culprit. So, to ensure security of cables:

- Install proper trunking and conduits for cables to lie in.
- Consider moving to 10/100 Base T cabling, if for no other

reason than the fact that a single lose or broken cable need not bring down an entire network.

- Ensure that there is adequate slack between the cable socket and the computer base, there should be no strain on the cabler.
- Ensure that cable connectors are in good condition.
- Be aware of the fact that installation next to electricity cables or equipment *may* cause unwanted interference, this can also be caused by fluorescent lighting.
- Ensure that the cable runs are documented, and are regularly checked for unauthorized connection of equipment to a network.
- If you are using a network that has wireless communication media, rather than cabling, then ensure that you are encrypting data transmission. There are well-documented instances where people have used out-of-the-box deployments of wireless networking, and have discovered that their network traffic is being intercepted by third parties. Interception can even occur outside of buildings, from the adjacent street!

7.2.7 Notebooks and other portable equipment

Designed to be portable and carried easily, laptops pose a considerable threat to network security. Yet this fact is seldom considered by many that use notebook computers. There have been several high-profile reports in the press of notebook computers being stolen from their owners that have contained information of the highest level of classification. The consequences of that information being compromised could be extremely serious. More usually, in the case of a laptop being stolen, the loss of one's work if not backed up is at a personal level inconvenient to say the least. Yet, based on the continued occurrence of these incidents of theft, there does not appear to be any re-evaluation of the risk by laptop users. In order to reduce the risk or impact of laptop theft, the following actions should be taken.

- Any work carried out on a laptop should carry minimal impact, commercial or otherwise, if lost or divulged by accident.
- Ensure that information stored on the laptop is also stored on the server, and that correct revision control is used to ensure work is kept up to date.
- Partition the hard drive in the laptop. Store any data required

while disconnected from the server, perhaps while working at home or on the move, in the second partition away from the operating system files and application programs in the first partition. This has two benefits: first, should the operating system crash or require reinstallation data integrity is preserved; second, the latter partition can be encrypted if required, providing some degree of security in the event of theft.

- Carry the notebook in a bag that does not scream 'NOTE-BOOK FOR THE TAKING!' Opportunists might overlook your boring briefcase, and move to the next person with the modern leather look branded notebook case.
- If you need to send data across a network using remote access, then use some sort of encrypted data transfer if you consider the data to be in any way confidential.
- Beware of letting guests visiting your premises plug their notebooks into your network. Unless there is a good reason, don't let them! How well do you know the guest and what software tools are they using?

7.3 Personnel security

After you have dealt with physical security, the next area to consider is personnel security. This includes the appropriate control and vetting of the personnel who are administering, maintaining, or using your secure network.

7.3.1 Background checks and references

Should you have any information that is of real significance maybe you are involved in highly sensitive commercial work or your organization is part of, or is working for, the Government – then you should certainly consider vetting the background of your employees. In some cases, particularly with government work, this might be a mandatory requirement. If you do not already subject employees to vetting, then you may wish to employ vetting procedures yourself to check that prospective employees are not in debt, or have not got any history that might cast some doubt on their suitability for the job. The background check should not be done as a matter of course, but should be carried out according to the degree of risk involved with a particular job. In most cases, you would be wise to inform the interviewee or employee that such checks are being carried out. Of course, the checks should start with the validation of the candidate's CV. From this starting point, you should consider:

- Credibility of employment record.
- Credibility of qualifications.
- Credibility of the reasons for leaving previous employment.
- You might want to consider the person's lifestyle, though be aware that this is an extremely sensitive subject and should be tackled in an open, honest, and non-judgemental fashion.
- The degree of debt that an individual holds might be a consideration, certainly credit referencing is part of many government vetting schemes.
- Has the employee got a criminal record? If so, do the offences indicate the potential to cause breaches in future? Again, sensitivity and respect are crucial.

Of course, do consider that these options are not exhaustive, and that you might not wish to use all of these criteria in all cases.

Another point worth noting is that as individuals progress their career within an organization, so their exposure to sensitive information changes and therefore they may need to be subjected to additional vetting. Most governments have varying levels of security clearance, but many organizations do not. Over time, a staff member's need to access different types of information will change, and that need may not necessarily mean that access rights will increase. Finally, you should consider whether or not you need to provide a pass that discriminates between staff of varying clearance if you operate such a scheme.

7.3.2 Access to information and account privilege

In all cases, access to information and subsequent user account privilege must operate on a basis of 'need to know'. This flies in the face of the management style of many organizations which is transparent and open. But, transparency and openness should not, for instance, apply to payroll information.

Do bear in mind that your role as a security specialist within your organization is not to define these levels of clearance or access yourself, but to make your organization aware that such controls could be put in place. To summarize:

- Assess the access rights that an account carries on a periodic basis.

- Use account and group privilege to control access to information.
- Work on a basis of 'need to know', rather than 'want to know'.

7.4 Support procedures

Computers are complicated pieces of machinery and, as we all know, they can often go wrong, usually at the most inopportune moment. For this reason, organizations often invest heavily in providing an appropriate degree of technical support. Many of the causes of computer disruption and failure can be eliminated by the introduction of stricter security controls, as security is partly about the elimination of computer downtime as much as possible. Nevertheless, there will be occasions on any network when computers just 'go wrong'. This may be due to hardware failure, or might be due to a software bug. In either case, your security practices may not, with the best will in the world, be able to prevent such events from happening. For this reason, all employees need to be aware of the support framework.

7.4.1 Support framework, including helpdesk

The support framework should be constructed to provide timely and effective support to the user base within an organization, in order that maximum utility and availability may be derived from the network. To be effective, the support framework needs to be well planned out according to operational requirements, documented, adhered to by support staff, and understood and adhered to by the users.

The helpdesk, as the primary point of contact for support, needs to have a clearly defined role, and there needs to be a clear and well-understood decision process for problem solving which dictates whether problems are solved on the spot, or whether they are escalated. There are three observations pertinent to helpdesks:

- Ensure that the helpdesk staff are technically competent and can understand fully the nature of the user's problem. User frustration arises when the helpdesk merely adopts a secretarial role, documenting the problem and allotting a call number, and adding little value beyond that.
- This is because, in most instances, calls to the helpdesk are relating to problems that are fairly trivial, and can therefore be solved by a helpdesk staff member who has a good basic

knowledge. The most common helpdesk calls tend to be relating to recurring problems. Given that this is the case, helpdesk staff should be empowered to solve these simple and recurring problems.

- Of course, with regard to passwords, the helpdesk should take great care to establish whether calls regarding passwords are bona fide before they are addressed. Calling a user back at their designated extension might, before the problem is addressed, go some way to authenticating the request for password help, but this must be coupled with other controls. Social engineering, whereby the helpdesk is sweet-talked into divulging or resetting passwords, is one of the easiest ways of gaining access to a network system, with no need for any operating system cracking to have taken place.

7.4.2 Danger of peer support

One of the main dangers facing helpdesk is peer support. Often, the first thing many of us do is try to fix our computers ourselves or failing that, get our colleagues to have a look. Now, some organizations have instigated a system of part-time support where staff are given responsibility for network support alongside their normal duties. This part-time support can work fine most of the time, though I would not recommend this as a cost-effective way of providing support. This is because one of the problems with part-time support is that the support provider cannot be realistically expected to be kept abreast of configuration aspects of the computer or network that are particular to each organization. Moreover, configuration changes or problem solving often requires software installation disks, which are only held by the full-time support staff.

Peer support on the other hand is where a computer goes wrong and so the user calls on the help of their friends or colleagues, in an informal capacity, who will have no training or particular understanding of the organization's network. In such cases, there are two main dangers associated with peer support.

First, problems addressed by untrained peer support are often made rapidly worse, and get to a state where they cannot be resolved by the peer support providers, moreover, the computer is left in a worst state than before the problem was addressed. This leads to more actual downtime than would have been the case had proper support measures been called for.

Second, if through peer support, users begin to assume more responsibility for maintenance then there is no true point of accountancy when problems occur. Who assumes responsibility for a virus attack which occurred because a user forgot to install the latest virus guard update?

- Do not underestimate the time wasted through peer support. I have witnessed three people indulging in peer support for their hapless colleague, over a duration of two days. At that rate, the company would have been better off and would have actually saved money if they had just bought a new computer.
- Peer support should be actively discouraged. If you feel the case is particularly strong in your organization, peer support could be made a disciplinary offence.
- Peer support is often attempted because helpdesk support is seen to be inadequate. Do not give your users due cause to form this point of view.
- If necessary, resort to physical locking of the computer cases to prevent peer support.
- Ensure your workstations are using 32-bit Windows clients. Windows 95 or Windows 98, with their lack of file system access rights, are particularly easy for the peer supporter to mess up!

7.4.3 User account lifecycle

Support procedures should also be concerned with the day-to-day management of user accounts. The best way to manage accounts is by adopting a lifecycle approach, where there is a complete audit trail provided for account inception through to the deletion of the account, and of all the account changes in between.

Accounts need to be managed. Whenever an employee leaves the organization, the account that would normally be used by that employee then becomes redundant. If your organization has a high flux of employees, and is also a large organization, then after a few months there could be great many redundant accounts. Each redundant account offers a way in for someone wishing to gain unauthorized access. By virtue of being redundant, the account activity is unlikely to be noted, except by a particularly vigilant system administrator. Redundant accounts might also offer continued access to the departing employee, this is particularly true in the case of remote access facilities being offered. Also, email can accumulate in mail boxes, and in extreme cases, could cause denial of service by the hard disk filling up.

Account lifecycle management should be precipitated as a procedure either by yourself as a security specialist, or by the system administrators or the IT manager or director. This might take the form of additional paperwork to be completed on hiring and departure of employees, part of the plethora of paperwork that is administered by the personnel department. At the very least, there should be notification from personnel once an employee is hired in order that an account can be created, and again once an employee has departed. This alone should be the initiation for account creation and deletion.

- When employees move on, ensure that redundant accounts are deleted.
- Have an agreed policy for dealing with information and data within the account. Better to copy this to someone else and retain a backup rather than just leave the account dormant to 'keep the information safe'.
- Does email need to be auto-forwarded, or redirected to another employee within your organization?
- Instigate a lifecycle approach to account management, whereby account creation, activity, and subsequent deletion is initiated by appropriate instructions from personnel.

7.5 Secure configuration

The next stage of the security process is what is for many the real meat of the subject, configuration of the operating system in order to increase security. We shall cover the general principles here, rather than examine the individual features of each operating system. Although the pointers provided here are fairly simple to apply in each case and their application will tighten up security considerably, application within each operating system will vary. Visit your manuals, help files, or the vendor website for further details. Microsoft in particular has detailed information about the procedures for tightening security with their Windows product families on their website.

7.5.1 BIOS

The BIOS should have a password set so that system administrators can set the computer to boot from the hard drive only. The facility to boot from the floppy drive or from the CD-ROM should be disabled. Otherwise, the computer could be booted from the floppy drive and all the installed operating system security features bypassed in order to access the hard drive. Some thought should be given to the securing of computer cases, which are often designed to be opened without any tools.

Inside, on the motherboard, is a switch that can be used to bypass or reset the password. This should of course be inaccessible to users.

That done, we can move onto the actual operating system. The main principles of secure operating system configuration can be summarized as follows:

- Network services, configured to running essential services only.
- Permission and group control.
- Authentication through password control.

Let's review these in turn.

7.5.2 Network services, essential services only

The first principle in securing a computer, particularly a network server, is to install and operate only the particular network services that the computer host is intended to be offering. The rationale for this statement is due to the fact that:

- Each service requires a listening port to be open.
- Each service installed is likely to have vulnerabilities that can be exploited to compromise a host's integrity. These vulnerabilities may be known or unknown at the time of installation.
- Each service consumes resources such as memory, CPU time, disk space, etc.
- Each service generates a log file reporting service activity. The verbosity of the reporting can be tailored to suit, though the more services there are, the more complex the log file report.

The first step when installing an operating system within a network environment should be to ascertain which services are required. This will be relatively easy in most instances, for instance a Web server will be providing HTTP services, and will therefore require a server application such as Apache or Microsoft IIS. An email server will be providing SMTP services, so will require SendMail or Microsoft Exchange. An office file server will most likely be a base installation of Windows with nothing much else besides.

Once you are clear about the services you will want to offer, you must then establish how to disable or uninstall the services you do not wish to provide. This is an important point to note, because many out-of-the-box default operating system installations provide many more services by default than you actually require. For example, if you were planning to host Microsoft Exchange on a Windows server, then you would most likely be well advised to disable or better still not to install all the other network services that are also installed by default. This will save resources and lessen the chance of exploitation of those server application vulnerabilities.

How can you determine what services are installed? Well, there are two ways. First, you could use a port scanner that will give instant results and will be similar to those a cracker might obtain. Second, you can log on and then examine the processes running on the computer. In the case of Unix hosts, you can use the top command, or the ps command, while in the case of Windows you can use the Task Manager. In short, the best policy is to deny services until they are explicitly required.

7.5.3 Permissions and groups

The next step is to examine the permissions and groups associated with each user account. Permissions and groups enable access controls to be placed upon individual files so that only certain accounts are able to access certain files. In this way the operating system files are able to be protected from casual inspection by ordinary users, while the administrator is able to have access to all the files on the system so that administrative duties can be carried out.

The concept of account permissions is fairly simple, but may not be familiar to users of a single user operating system such as Windows 95 or 98. Within a network operating system, such as Windows or Unix, each user account is assigned a unique identifier. Users are able to manipulate files that they have created themselves and that are stored in their user directory. Users are also able to read, execute, write to, or delete, other files within the operating system depending on the controls set by the system administrator, or those controls installed by default. This is useful because you may not want anyone else to be able to read documents you are working on, so these can be stored within your own directory which can be made inaccessible to other users.

Group permissions are less widely understood and offer some additional control over user privileges. Groups can be used in the same way as account permissions, to assign write, read, and execute status to various users and files. An advantage of groups is that they can be used to assign rights to whole groups of users at once. For instance, there may be a software application that is only to be used by certain users, such as a financial package. This software application could then be configured to be used by a defined group, such as finance, and then all permitted users could be assigned as members of that group.

The best way of setting up account and group permissions is according to the 'need to know' principle. Beware, though, when changing system files from the default permissions. If you change permissions inappropriately, you could lock yourself out of the system, even as system administrator! You would be well advised to follow a guide, such as those available from vendor security Web pages, and test the configuration on a lab computer before making any changes to your operational servers and workstations.

7.5.4 User account names and passwords

User account names and passwords are one of the most import-ant aspects of network security. This is because the first line of attack for anyone wishing to gain unauthorized access to a host will almost certainly be a password controlled authentication process. A weak password will quite simply be an inadequate defence against all but the most casual cracker.

Quite often passwords can be cracked by simple guesswork, on the basis of the user's name, their beloved's name, their pet's names, their hobbies, likes, interests, address, postal code or zip code, etc. But, even if passwords are strong enough to withstand simple guesswork, and there are some determined people willing to spend a great deal of time researching and guessing likely passwords, then there are a plethora of automated pass-word crackers available which are more than up to the job.

To combat password guessing, many operating systems have the ability to lock a user account after a predetermined number of unsuccessful attempts. This has the effect of rejecting all subsequent attempts to log on to the locked account. As soon as a password has been cracked open, then the relevant user account is breached and the intruder is able to snoop around the operating system files and look for aspects of the system that make the system vulnerable to further attack. The aim of most crackers is to gain the administrator account's password, and therefore access to the administrator privileges.

So, the best way to prevent casual cracking of accounts is to ensure that passwords are chosen so as to provide some sort of resistance to the casual attempt, and ensure that account logins are monitored for repeated failures, which might indicate a break-in attempt has taken place. One point to note is that password authenticated Web directories, those password protected parts of some websites, usually have no such system in place.

Account names

Bearing the aforementioned in mind, what is the best advice for account names? Well, in most cases, accounts are named after the person who uses them. This is de-facto normal practice, and is acceptable providing that each account is sufficiently protected by a password due to the relative ease with which account names can be guessed.

If security of your accounts is a big concern, then you should consider using some sort of arbitrary naming policy for your accounts. This will ensure that account names cannot be deduced from the name of the person who normally uses that account or from their email address. The downside is that users will, in the short term, find such an arbitrary account naming policy difficult to adapt to.

Passwords

More important than the account naming policy, though, is the password policy. Passwords should be chosen so that they are obscure and difficult to guess. A good password will have the following features:

- The password shall not be a derivative of the user account name.
- The password shall not be a dictionary word in any language.
- None of the above shall be used in conjunction with a numerical prefix or suffix.
- The password shall contain upper and lower case characters.
- The password shall contain a mix of numerical and alphabet characters and perhaps some control characters if you are really keen to protect the account.
- The password shall be easy to type and easy to remember.

How many passwords do you know which fulfil these criteria? Very few indeed, most probably.

One of your biggest challenges as a security administrator will be getting users to start using passwords which are more secure, and as far as they are concerned, more difficult to remember. You will most likely wish to draw up your own

individual password policy, and couple this with some configuration changes in your account manager tool for whichever
operating system you are using. To facilitate this process, in
most cases, users should be able to choose passwords for
themselves, based upon the above criteria, and following some
degree of password education. The only exception to this rule
would be where account security is deemed of sufficient
importance that strong passwords be generated by some automated method.

Once passwords have been chosen, then users should be
encouraged to ensure that the password remains secure.
Passwords should be changed frequently, particularly those
passwords used with secure systems that have confidential or
sensitive information. The frequency with which users should
change their password can be enforced by the administrator and
can be varied from months to hours according to the needs of
the organization.

The system administrators should ensure that the password
policy is being maintained, though this might sound difficult if
users are assigning passwords to their own accounts. The
answer is to conduct regular patrols of the password file, not
with the niceties of an administrator but using the same
methods as a cracker. In particular, run a password cracking
tool on your computer, having copied or obtained the password file from the server. Are you surprised at how quick
some of the passwords are cracked? Also, check for evidence of
recording of passwords on pieces of paper near the workstations.

7.5.5 Default accounts

Be aware that Windows and Unix contain default account
names for the administrator and sometimes for guest users as
well. These default user names are dangerous. They allow a
casual cracker to detect the administrative accounts or even to
login to the operating system or password protected services,
often with no additional work if default passwords are used.

All default named accounts should be renamed, using the
same naming convention as other user accounts. In addition
you may wish to create dummy accounts that are locked out to
act as decoys or substitutes to the real thing. Default account
names include the 'Administrator' account in Windows operating systems and 'root' in Unix systems.

The policies outlined above can be readily implemented
within the account management utilities of most operating

systems. When you install your operating system you should configure the user accounts along the following lines:

- Lock the account after a defined number of repetitive unsuccessful logins.
- Require the users to change their password at regular intervals, decided upon in the context of your operating environment.
- Require users to use successively different passwords each time their password is changed.
- If necessary, and certainly if evidence of one of the password utilities suggests so, strong password selection should be enforced using software tools. This prevents the user from choosing dictionary words as passwords, or passwords like 'QWERTY'.

Whatever changes you choose to make to your operating systems, there are two points to bear in mind, though, before you start making any changes.

- First, try out these configuration changes on your lab system and certainly not on a live network until you are confident you can attain the effect you require.
- Second, be aware that each organization will have individual security requirements, so do not feel you need to implement all of the suggestions contained here, just the ones you feel will have a benefit.

7.6 Review

- Address physical security first, paying attention to the security of the operational environment, the security of the servers and desktop computers, and of associated network hardware.
- Notebook protection deserves particular attention with regard to the prevention of theft and the protection of any sensitive data stored on the device.
- Personal checks should be considered for staff working with sensitive data.
- Ensure that information is available on a 'need to know' basis.
- Document support procedures, and discourage peer support.
- Establish procedures for the creation and deletion of user accounts.
- Set BIOS passwords, ensuring cases cannot be opened easily.
- Run essential network services only.
- Set permissions and groups according to the 'need to know' rule.

- Ensure passwords are used appropriately.
- Pay attention to default accounts, rename and/or disable as appropriate.
- Configure user accounts to force password changes, lock the account after multiple attempts to log in.
- Follow the guidance available for details of the configuration of your specific operating system. This can often be found on vendor websites.

7.7 To do

7.7.1 Basic security checklist

- Tackle physical security prior to any other actions taken to secure your network. Pay attention to:
  1. Housing of the network servers and other equipment
  2. Access to network servers and other equipment. Should you have a swipecard or punch code lock?
  3 Install adequate air conditioning
  4 Ensure that fire extinguishers are CO_2, not water based
  5. Ensuring flooding is not a potential hazard
  6. Install appropriate UPS facilities
  7. Check cabling is securely routed. Close off any sockets that are not in use
  8. Install appropriate storage facilities for software
  9. Mark all hardware, and advertise the fact to deter theft
  10. Ensure computer cases cannot be opened easily to protect against tampering
  11. Issue non-obvious cases for employee's laptops, and ditch the vendor cases
  12. Control access to your premises. Issue visitor badges, and identity cards. Challenge strangers
- Instigate, in association with personnel, some form of background checking for employees working with sensitive data.
- Document support procedures, including points of contact and responsibility. Who should be contacted in the event of a virus?
- Establish a lifecycle for account management, from account creation to account deletion, and the allocation of account privilege. Ensure that personnel have input into the lifecycle.
- Which application services shall each of your servers be providing? Ensure that all other services are disabled.
- How will you use groups to segregate users?
- Encourage or enforce the use of strong passwords.
- Rename and disable the default accounts.

- Ensure that accounts are made resilient to repeat attempts to log on by invoking account lockout after a maximum number of unsuccessful login attempts.
- Visit the website of your vendor and locate secure installation checklists. For instance, there is a checklist for the secure installation of Windows NT4 that walks you through the complete process with step-by-step instructions at each stage.

8

Acceptable use

A survey published by IDC Research, stated that an average of 30–40 per cent of Internet access from within the corporate workplace was not business related.

A great deal of attention concerning network security is focused primarily on the technical aspects, on software and hardware configuration, and on appropriate technical solutions such as firewalls and content management. Of course, this leaves one important variable out of the equation, the users of the network, and as a consequence, what we would term 'the people issues'.

This chapter discusses the people issues, or the subject of acceptable use, a topic for debate that will be encountered at some time or another within any organization. Often, examination of acceptable use raises two points: first, *acceptable use issues are not always security issues per se*, sometimes they are personnel issues; second, *there are no formulaic or prescriptive rules for defining acceptable use* that will suit every organization's needs.

Because of this lack of clearly understood definition, there is a temptation to search for technical solutions with which to tackle acceptable use. This is too simplistic an approach to take, however. Before technical solutions can be deployed effectively, a clear policy directive needs to be arrived at in order that technical solutions reflect the thinking of your organization. What constitutes acceptable use in your organization should be determined in consultation with all the stakeholders, and certainly with input from the IT department, from line management, and also from the personnel department.

8.1 The notion of acceptable use

Acceptable use defines the parameters and constraints with which an organization's computers and other network resources shall be used by employees of that organization. These parameters and constraints are often contained in the form of guidance within an acceptable use policy. Organizations will often have one of two main motives for drawing up a policy. First, there is the perceived need to protect the security of the network, much in the same way as a security policy may do. Or, there is the perceived need to address personnel issues such as perceived time wasting on computers or viewing inappropriate (not necessarily unlawful) content on the Web. The two motives are slightly different. The former is a direct concern, the latter is perhaps not.

For IT staff, moot point is: 'Should we (as members of the IT department, say, or even specifically as security experts) be concerned with personnel matters associated with misuse of the computer network?' Well, in short, yes.

- The first reason is that despite the personnel dimension of some misuse problems, they are *perceived* to be network security problems. Because users surf the Web, and the Web is accessed via the company network, then the problem lies with IT. Yes, this is a bit like blaming the telecom provider for those calls to Australia made every so often. But, as most managers are aware of the fact that there are technology measures that can be put in place, solving the problem will fall to IT sooner or later in any case. Better to be involved up front with setting a sensible policy for acceptable use, rather then implement a badly planned policy, enforced using technical solutions, with misplaced expectations, as a result of a knee jerk response from the senior management.
- Second, a culture of pervasive misuse can lead to some degree of real threat to the secure network. This threat could be in the form of potential exposure of the organization to unwanted legal attention or publicity if nothing else. Downloading Page 3 may not be illegal, but forwarding those pictures to female employees may constitute harassment. The possibility of reducing the likelihood of this type of threat occurring is the most compelling reason for acceptable use to be part of the security policy and for the security administrator to have input into addressing acceptable use issues.

But, we should not lose sight of the fact that people with too much time on their hands, and therefore the opportunity to surf the Web all day, remains a personnel issue about performance expectation within the organization and associated work load. This should never become an IT issue or a network security issue.

Anticipating and defining the security threats that could arise from the personnel aspect of acceptable use is the key to making policy. When defining acceptable use, therefore, a good start would be to examine the salient points contained within the various legislative Acts, and then seek guidance from your legal department, or similar. The best way to reduce the likelihood of the law being broken is to make specific reference to these Acts. This will educate the user community and illustrate the point that many aspects of acceptable use are not instances of the organization being unduly authoritarian, but are in place in order to ensure compliance with the law. Some of the main aspects of acceptable use are itemized below.

8.1.1 Libel

Acceptable use should include taking care not to libel competitor companies, or individuals, by email or by the Web. Cases of libel that have occurred on the Internet are heard in the courts every year. Yet despite the media attention given to each case, organizations do not appreciate the fact the libel laws apply to the Internet. Defining what is and what is not libellous can sometimes be a costly and time-consuming exercise, but common sense often dictates. For more information, read the Defamation Act 1996.

8.1.2 Data Protection

The obligation to be compliant with the Data Protection Act 1998 will have an impact on a relatively small group of users, such as the marketing department, for example, but the limited numbers of users affected should not mean that the importance of compliance is relegated. The Act is clear in that if you collect and process personal data within your company systems, you must inform data subjects of your reasons for wishing to do so, and obtain their permission. This applies to all forms of marketing, including the gathering of information from within websites.

8.1.3 Indecency

Mention the Internet and many people think about indecency, an emotive subject that is a good enough reason for some to 'ban the Internet' altogether! Of course, the problem is that any informed person knows that the Internet is indeed rife with indecent or pornographic images, found in the main on the Web and within the news groups, but on occasions distributed by email between friends and colleagues. But the emotive nature of indecency should not prevent the issue from being dealt with in a measured fashion. Inaction, either by you as the security administrator, or by your organization's senior management, may in turn lead to adverse publicity for your organization or even prosecution of some of your staff.

There are cases reported in the media with regular occurrence of organizations dismissing several users for downloading and swapping pictures. But, there is a feeling that some of these instances are perhaps an over-reaction on behalf of the organizations involved who have, until such decisive action was taken, made little effort to educate their employees. If we are to avoid getting side-tracked into tackling the issue through invoking arguments of time wasting, which is a personnel issue, then the main problem in defining policy lies in the definition of what is indecent. But, not even the law is entirely clear on this and public attitudes, which to an extent shape the legal view, i.e. with reference to the Obscene Publications Act, are also changing.

As a guideline to what is indecent, you might consider whether or not you would find the same sorts of image concerned in a newspaper or perhaps a magazine? If not, because of the explicit content of the image, then the image is probably indecent. Many organizations, though, broaden this rule of thumb definition to include Page 3 or Maxim and this is when the problem starts. Do you ban the tabloid press or the majority of popular magazines from the workplace as well? Furthermore, would you dismiss someone for reading these publications in their lunch hour? Probably not.

Although people agree that indecent images in the workplace is an issue that must be tackled, most people do not agree on how. Let's clarify the problem domain and define just what sorts of questions must be answered while deciding on a policy that can control the downloading of images.

The pursuit of pornography (in the legal sense of the word) on the Internet should be seen as a security issue for the following reasons:

- The network resources are misused, in extreme cases gigabytes of storage capacity are lost.
- The possession and publication of pornographic material is illegal.
- The investigation of offences committed can entail the shutting down of computer hardware that is suspected of being involved.

In terms of drafting acceptable use policy, then, you will need to ask the following questions:

- How are you going to define what images are appropriate to store on your network and what are not?
- Are you willing to extend the criteria you have used in the above questions to other media used in your organization?
- Are you willing to ban all images from being stored on the network, except those that are used for the organization's purposes?
- Are you willing to curtail, monitor or even ban the use of the Web, email, and news groups?

The perpetual downloaders will be caught out sooner or later, and in any case, most people will take their cue on whether or not to download indecent pictures and keep them on their hard drive from the prevalent attitude to security within their organization. If they feel that they could not get away with having megabytes of disk space being used for indecent images, they probably won't bother trying.

When you are clear on your answers to the above questions, then you can turn to the technology to help enforce your policy. You can use content security applications, looked at later in the book, or you can filter website URLs, as part of the firewall policy. News groups should also be filtered. Just be aware that the stricter your policy, the more difficult the policy will be to enforce. You might find that the best way forward is to educate users about the legal arguments and ensure employees are aware of the risks to them and to the organization if indecent material is stored on, or sent to and from, your network.

8.2 Uncontrolled software

Most likely, you will be concerned with reducing the threats due to viruses, and to this end will have installed virus protection on your computer networks. This is because, by and large, viruses are propagated on the Internet. But, storage media such as CD-

ROMs and floppy disks remain as potential sources of infection. For this reason many acceptable use policies specifically prohibit the use of third party software. This may include bona fide software owned by the user, limited trial, shareware or freeware found on magazine cover disks, or software that has been downloaded from the Internet.

Another important reason for the prohibition of third party software is that software installed without prior examination and testing in a controlled environment cannot be guaranteed to coexist in a stable fashion with all the other authorized software on a workstation computer. Installation of badly designed software could change configuration files, such as the registry, to the detriment of the computer's stability. Certainly, the addition of more and more additional software will consume system resources. Although correlation does not imply cause, many computers that are found to be running slow, or are prone to intermittent crashing, tend to have large amounts of third party software installed by users, particularly shareware from magazine cover disks.

Then, there are certain types of software that you would not wish any user to be using, and that is the software that can be found in the 'Tools of the trade' chapter earlier in the book. Software, such as network analysers, or port scanners, has a use by administrators, or by crackers, but not by the average office user, unless they fall into the latter category. Such software should be explicitly banned within an acceptable use policy.

Users should also be discouraged from installing third party software, whether purchased by themselves or downloaded from the Internet. But, there are occasions when software can be obtained that is in fact useful and well worth having. Web browsers, document readers such as Adobe Acrobat, and software services and patches are three such instances.

What is needed is a controlled way in which software can be downloaded by system administrators, upon the request of users, and then distributed in a controlled and tested fashion. The company intranet might be the best place to freely distribute software for installation, but even so, installation should perhaps be carried out by administrators.

- The procedure for distribution and installation of such useful utilities should be documented in the acceptable use policy.

8.3 Personal use

To be honest, most of us have at one time or another used our employers' computers for private purposes while at work, that is to say we have used computers in ways unconnected with our role or job function. Often, we will try and legitimize such use by saying that we are taking a break or that we are using the computer in our own time. Most employers see private use rather differently, though, and would term such use unproductive or a waste of resources.

Again, we should resist being led into solving personnel issues of workload and productivity through acceptable use policy. Our primary aim is not to police people's working habits. In any case, many of the instances of private use can be dealt with in a security context by appeal to legal use or use of uncontrolled software. For example, wasting time sending pictures to colleagues might in an extreme case constitute publication of pornography, as well as being unproductive. Similarly, downloading and playing games might constitute using uncontrolled software, as well as being unproductive.

But some instances are not so readily qualified. What about browsing the Web for the last minute holiday deals? Or, what about sending email to relatives or friends outside of the organization? Neither instance constitutes a breach of network security, yet on the other hand, neither is a productive use of the organization's time or computer network. Certainly, browsing the Web for holiday deals is probably not going to cause anyone any headache from a security perspective. In fact, one might argue that the more employees understand of ecommerce and the Web, the better. The same case can be said of the email user, but with one caveat. Too much personal use of email could lead to undesirable use, through there being a de-facto 'anything goes' policy. Sending mail to relatives and friends, becomes forwarding the latest jokes, which then leads to the latest pictures. Personal use should not be prohibited within a security context, but users should be very clear about what constitutes *acceptable* personal use.

8.4 Acceptable use of email

Even though the Web has arguably been the catalyst for the Internet's tremendous expansion, email remains the staple application for the Internet. Messages are quick to type, are usually written informally, and can be sent very quickly. Also, email offers a convenient way of sending documents to colleagues.

Recently, though, email has proven to be a far more dangerous medium than most have come to assume. Email poses several problems:

- Viruses can be propagated by email attachment.
- There is the security aspect of email in that, like a facsimile, you never really know who will receive the message. A great many managers still have their email printed out by their PA staff, for instance.
- Email has the same legal standing, within many jurisdictions, as other forms of written communication. This has certainly been demonstrated in the UK. Therefore, users should take great care when sending email. The fact is that written communication by email should be regarded with the same attention and gravity as that of a letter sent on company headed paper.

Most organizations have woefully inadequate measures in place to prevent the most unsuitable email messages being sent, in effect, on behalf of the organization. When you consider that the organization from where an email originated can be easily identified, usually by the domain name of the email address, and sometimes from the signature file, one wonders how much longer this situation will continue. Certainly, few organizations would countenance permitting employees to send personal letters, of any kind, on headed paper, so why should organizations permit email to be used for anything else other than business communications? To delineate the use of email clearly, acceptable use of email might therefore include the following mandatory rules:

- Email should be used for communications on behalf of the organization only.
- Only documents associated with the organization should be attached to outgoing emails.
- Email should not contain material or discussion that is classified or sensitive.
- Email should be proof read and spell-checked prior to sending.
- Finally, users should be informed that in most cases, their user account identity and that of the organization are contained in the email message sent.

8.4.1 Use of disclaimers on email

Many organizations use a standard disclaimer, that is a short piece of text inserted automatically into the foot of each email. This is written in order to absolve responsibility for any unlawful or contentious content within the email. The thinking behind the disclaimer is that even though the organization's email system is being used, the email is being composed by an individual and the organization as a whole is not responsible for that individual's actions. In practice, however, there is no legal standing to these disclaimers, and certainly not within the UK.

Many organizations continue to use disclaimers, though, as this arguably imposes *some* obligation on the recipient, which *could* add weight to a case brought before a court if information was subsequently misused. Perhaps there is a case for placing these disclaimers at the start of a message, so that this is read first and the recipient has a chance not to continue reading if they wish. *Nevertheless, the considered view of many within the legal profession is that disclaimers have little if any real value within the UK.*

8.5 Acceptable use of Usenet news

The advantages of Usenet news are that some of the news groups can be a very valuable resource, particularly so for computer administrators, programmers, or other IT profes-sionals, providing a prompt online source of user support and advice. This is true in particular for the comp.news hierarchy.

Usenet news is very similar to email in that the style and manner of composition is brief and informal and, like email, Usenet news, can be sent quickly and easily. Also, like email, news messages are very visible and provide an audit trail from the sender's organization to the particular news server they are stored on. For this reason, users should be guarded when writing news messages about particular issues within their organization. On no account should users include detailed information regarding the configuration of their network within messages, as this could almost be an invitation to crackers to test out their skills.

Problems also arise with regard to content on various news groups. A great deal of the news group content by way of text or images can be considered to be inappropriate. This is particu-larly evident in the alt.news hierarchy. Users should be informed about what is acceptable and what is not acceptable when viewing news messages. The problems posed by cross-posting in many of the unmoderated news groups means that many unconnected news groups often contain inappropriate material, the presence of which will be clearly evident to the user. Acceptable use for Usenet news can be expressed in terms of the following points

- Do not include organization or company specific information within news group postings.
- Do not download material that appears to be illegal, even if found in news groups that have little to do with the offending material.
- System administrators should provide news groups on a case by case basis, upon request from users.

8.6 Acceptable use of the Web

At last, we get to what in many organizations' view is the main source of problems with the Internet, the World Wide Web. For those organizations, the Web is not only an essential part of the wired economy, but also a means for many staff to idle away the hours when they should be engaged in productive work.

Ensuring that staff are working productively is, as alluded to earlier, not our issue for the time being, but is a line management issue or personnel issue. There is clear legal precedent for taking appropriate courses of action, including dismissal, for spending longer than is deemed acceptable while using the Web. Surfing the Web does become a security issue, however, when inappropriate, offensive or illegal material is being browsed or downloaded, or when shareware is being downloaded and installed. To this end, users again need to be educated about the acceptability of material that can be found on the World Wide Web, and that availability of material does not imply that such material is acceptable. This is an aspect of the Web that should not be overlooked – some estimates put the number of inappropriate Web documents as constituting more than 80 per cent of Web traffic being downloaded by employees while at work.

Downloading and installation of software from the Web should also be discouraged. This is because installing software in an uncontrolled and untested environment often leads to various complications, including risk of virus infection, and the risk of badly configured or installed third party software modifying the desktop computer's configuration. Moreover, users are not best prepared to remedy any problems they may cause, and often the most time effective method of solving problems is for a reinstallation of the operating system and other software applications.

Given that users should be discouraged from browsing through inappropriate websites, or from downloading software, there is arguably no reason why the Web should not be used for personal browsing. The best way of becoming an informed user of the Web is by plenty of practice, just so long as surfing is not done at the cost of productivity.

Particular attention might need to be given to whether or not users should be permitted to use their personal web-based email accounts within the workplace, such as hotmail or yahoo mail. These types of accounts can be a way of avoiding compliance with acceptable use email policies. Also, you may prevent certain documents from being sent by email attachment through your organization's email system, but the same document may well be able to be sent using web-based email. For this reason, and the possibility of escalating personal use, you might be advised to discourage the use of web-based email services by users.

To summarize, organizations should permit the use of the Web for personal or operational use subject to the following constraints:

- No viewing or downloading of inappropriate material.
- No downloading and installation of software.
- Discouraging the use of web-based email.

8.7 Use of passwords

No apology is made for repeating some of the points made earlier, as passwords are one of the most important parts of a networked computer's defences. Passwords are generally the first obstacle any cracker or unauthorized user will meet, and once compromised further access to a system is usually not difficult. Emphasis on passwords is also important in this context of acceptable use because they are one of the few areas of system security that individual users have a great degree of individual leverage over. All the best security in the world is reduced considerably if the password chosen to protect an account is woefully inadequate. For this reason, users should be educated about the correct choice of passwords. To recap, a good password will share these features.

- The password will not be derivative of the user name.
- The password will not be a dictionary word in any language.

- None of the above should be used in conjunction with a numerical prefix or suffix.
- The password will contain upper and lower case characters.
- The password will contain a mix of numerical and alphabet characters and perhaps some control characters.
- The password will be easy to type and easy to remember.

Anyone who is found to be setting weak passwords should be cautioned, and asked to set stronger passwords, using the points itemized above for guidance. Users should be encouraged to set their own passwords in all but the most demanding of security environments, being more likely to recall a password they have created themselves, than a password that has been set by the administrator. Recall that one of the main reasons for calling the helpdesk is to reset passwords.

8.8 Private use

Anyone working with secure information will be taking security seriously and will certainly be interested in preventing the information they are working with from falling into wrong hands or being deleted. How many users though will take measures to ensure that the casual observer cannot see the information they are working with displayed on their computer monitor either while in use, or worse still while unattended?

This is not as trivial as you think. Certainly anyone working within the defence sector will be taking this seriously, as will some working in the finance sector. Inadvertently allowing the casual observer to view a computer monitor could have extreme ramifications and should be considered in the same context as the clear desk policy that is in force in many of these organizations. There are several ways to prevent the casual observer from seeing the monitor.

While not in use, all computers should have their screens locked by using a screensaver with password protection enabled. This fulfils two requirements. First, the computer cannot be accessed while unattended and second the contents of the screen can be rendered invisible when not being used. The best way of using the screen lock is to set the screen lock to be triggered after some moderately short period of inactivity, say five minutes. In this way the screen lock will automatically turn on even if you forget to lock the screen yourself. The 'Blank' setting in some screensavers should not be used. If you are away from your computer for some time then you may think the computer has been turned off. When you try to turn the computer on again, you will in fact be shutting the computer off without shutting down the operating system, which can have a damaging effect on your file systems.

If you are concerned about the casual user, then you will almost certainly want to sit away from a facing window. This is not as daft as you might think. First of all bear in mind that with a pair of high power binoculars, anyone could view your monitor at a distance given the right vantage point. In this way, a computer monitor could be visible from some distance, even through glass. This fact has caused organizations that are concerned about security to install special windows that pass light one way only or to buy some blinds for their windows, sometimes only after having caught people with binoculars trying to look inside.

8.9 Review

- The notion of acceptable use defines the parameters and constraints within which an organization's computers and network resources should be used by employees. Many aspects of acceptable use are arguably personnel issues that should be dealt with HR, but because they involve computers, are seen to be problems that should be dealt with by the IT staff.
- Many of the parameters for acceptable use can be derived from the law, which makes the case for compliance with acceptable use far more compelling. Instances of such acceptable use guidelines include the downloading and distribution of inappropriate images, and use of personal data.
- Email should be written in the same style as any other formal written communications made on company headed paper. Care needs to be taken with the handling of email attachments, with guidance included in the acceptable use policy.
- Disclaimers should be used, but bearing in mind that their legal standing has yet to be established and that the considered view is that they are ineffective.
- Use of the Web should be encouraged for business purposes, and some organizations may choose to permit personal use of the Web subject to constraints regarding inappropriate material, downloading software and use of web-based email.
- Guidance for use of passwords should be part of the acceptable use policy.
- Use of password protected screensavers should be encouraged.

8.10 To do

8.10.1 Establish what constitutes acceptable use in your organization

- In conjunction with personnel, ascertain what constraints should be placed on a computer and Internet use within your organization. Remember that the more constraints you impose, the more difficult acceptable use will be to monitor.
- Educate employees about the legal framework pertaining to computer and Internet use, and use this as the foundation for policy.
- Are you going to allow uncontrolled software to be installed by employees?
- Are you going to permit personal use? What is the considered view of line management and personnel?
- Consider how employees should be using email and the Web. Will you allow email to be used for private communication or reserve email use for business purposes only?
- Promote the use of password protected screen locks.

9

Business continuity

Business continuity planning is much more than disaster recovery –
it is a strategic tool which, when understood, exercised well and with
commitment from all members of a business, can enhance flexibility
and improve competitiveness.

(Adair Turner, former Director-General of the CBI,
writing in *Business Continuity Management*,
published by Adam Associates)

Business continuity planning is focused on providing an organization with the ability to continue day-to-day operations in the
event of adverse conditions or disaster, which could lead to the
closure or even loss of the working premises. In such events,
new premises, new hardware, new telephone systems, can all be
arranged, but the unique asset to any organization is the data.
Central to business continuity is the ability to restore data in the
event of any disaster, big or small.

The importance of data backup and the need for effective
recovery of that data if required is well understood. At the most
trivial level, if a user accidentally deletes one of their files, most
system administrators are confident they can restore the missing
file. This is because after a period of trial and error, there have
been enough instances of accidental file deletion for an effective
recovery from that 'disaster' to be made. At the other end of the
scale, there is the need for the system administrator, indeed the
entire organization, to be able to recover from disaster that
renders the network or premises useless. This type of situation
is an order of magnitude more serious. Disasters do not occur

frequently, so there is little opportunity to learn from experience. In the absence of experience, organizations need to plan their strategy for continuing business operations when disaster strikes, and subject these plans to the scrutiny of regular rehearsal.

This chapter examines data backup and recovery as part of the larger issue of business continuity. Data backup and restoration strategies are reviewed, followed by discussion of business continuity planning as a means of reducing the effects of disaster on business operations in the event of worst case scenario – entire loss of business systems and data together with working premises.

9.1 Data is your most valuable asset

The value of data can be measured in terms of the effort invested in creating the data and the cost of not being able to access the data. Let's review the main reasons why data held on a network server or workstation is valuable to our organization:

- The amount of effort required producing the data.
- The amount of time required recreating the data if lost.
- Delay incurred as a result of data loss and the subsequent impact that would have on a project or business system.

When all of these factors are considered, the loss of data could have a significant impact on your organization. In most cases, the data is irreproducible. For many organizations, then, and particularly service-oriented organizations, data could be measured as one of their most valuable assets. Good data backup and restoration is therefore an essential requirement.

9.2 What can go wrong?

There are many reasons why data can be lost. How many of the instances below have you encountered?

9.2.1 User error

Possibly the most common reason for data loss is user error. Most users have accidentally deleted important files and then have been unable to recover the file. But, if proper data restoration procedures are in place, then the impact of user error is limited.

9.2.2 Administrative error

Perhaps not so common as user error (so we'd all like to think), but system administrators will make mistakes from time to time. In the event of inadvertently deleting a user's files, there needs to be an efficient means of recovering from that mistake. Administrators cannot pass the buck and remind the user of the need for regular backups!

9.2.3 Hardware failure

Computer hardware is often sold on the basis of having a limited lifetime, so you should not expect hardware to last forever. When hardware fails unexpectedly, there should be some plan of replacement that causes minimum disruption. Hardware may be subject to failure by user or administrative error, or just by wearing out prematurely and unexpectedly.

9.2.4 Operating system failure

Data loss can also arise each time a computer crashes. Operating systems such as Unix and Windows use virtual memory that provides an extension to the physical ram. The virtual memory is stored on the hard drive in a swap file or swap partition. Should a server crash then the memory files in the swap could be left in an unreadable state when the computer is rebooted. Consequences range from the mild, such as loss of a file, to a complete loss of server functionality such that the system has to be rebuilt. UPS provision will reduce the incidence of this particular threat.

9.2.5 Virus attacks

Should a virus infect computers, restoration of files to a state prior to infection may be required. Such restoration can only be carried out if proper backups are maintained.

9.3 Data backup

Does all the above sound a bit obvious? Probably, but you can probably recall instances when people have not backed up their data files as well as they should have done, or worse still have not backed up their data at all! Data backup is never interesting until you need to restore lost data. The principle of data backup is simple:

- Copy important data onto a removable storage medium or device.
- Then store the backed-up data somewhere safe and secure, but readily accessible to authorized users.
- In the event of data loss or unavailability, copy data back to the original or alternative location.

Constraints to this process are the amount of data to be copied, the storage capacity of the media, the speed and reliability of the restoration, and finally the cost of the whole process.

9.3.1 Backup plans

There are two aspects to consider concerning backups. First, should the backup be of all the files on a network server, or just some of the files such as users' data? Second, should backups be incremental backups or total backups?

Regarding the files to be copied, the first school of thought is that backups should be made of the data that is unique to the organization, such as user data files, application data files, and any other unique information stored by users on their computer workstations or servers. Instances of such data include all the documents that a user creates, in addition to the data created by the administrator such as password files, configuration files, patches, tweaks, etc. Effective data backup therefore relies upon all the unique information on the server or workstation computer being identified and subsequently copied to the backup media. When restoration is carried out, the operating system is installed, together with all the application software. Then, the unique data is copied back to the workstation or server so that restoration of the data environment is completed. The only problem with backing up data in this fashion is that the administrator must be able to identify, with confidence, each unique file. If only a few files are missing then the restoration will be incomplete.

The second school of thought is that a copy of the entire hard drive on the server should be taken and then stored on removable media, a disk image, as a means of backing up the operating system, software applications, user data and configuration files in one go. This may sound like more work in the first instance, but taking an entire disk image means that there is nothing missing from the subsequent restoration when the data is retrieved. In addition, the time taken to restore the disk image is often reduced when compared to restoration of unique data, because the element of operating system configuration is removed. The downside is that extra imaging software is required, to manage the backup and restoration process, and more media storage space is required, due to the lack of a facility to make incremental backups of user data.

Once the files to be backed up have been identified, you then need to consider the strategy for copying the files. The easier but more costly way to take a backup is to take a snapshot of the computer files identified for copying, by dumping them to a single backup file at some regular period. In Unix systems the tape archive command, tar, is often used to copy files onto removable tape. Administrators often choose to take such a backup each day, storing the tape in a safe place. The drawback with this type of plan is that an inordinate amount of backup media is required. Very few people would have the storage space for this backup plan.

Alternatively, incremental backups can be made. A full backup is carried out and the disk image is stored in a safe place. Then, after regular intervals, of say each day, an incremental backup is carried out of only those files that have been changed since the full backup was made. Then, after a fortnight or month, another full backup is made and kept in a safe place. The incremental backup is continued as normal, but the backup media can be reused from the last time. In this way, the amount of media used in the backup process is controlled, requiring less storage space. In addition, full backups should be made at irregular intervals to coincide with operating system upgrades, patches, etc. Be careful to reuse the oldest incremental backup media first, and then the remaining media in decreasing order of age. Do not use the newer media first; the most recent backups are those most likely to be used for restoration.

9.3.2 The right backup plan for your organization

To a great extent, the backup plan chosen for your organization will be tailored according to the:

- Type of organization.
- Operational and environmental circumstances.
- Dependency on data and information systems.
- Response times required in case of the need for data restoration either following localized data loss or disaster.

Generally speaking, the data recovery needs of a smaller office that uses information systems for word processing and spreadsheet analysis are far less demanding than those of a large merchant bank with several distributed back office information systems sharing data throughout offices around the world. These two very different businesses will have very different needs, when the criteria of media choice, reliability of restoration and speed of restoration are assessed.

9.3.3 Media choice

The main criteria for media to be used for data backup is that the media should be removable, able to be readily portable, able to be stored in large quantities, and have resilience. The capacity of the media is also an important consideration. Clearly, backing up an office server onto a floppy disk capacity of 1.44 MB is not viable, as too many disks would be required. A more appropriate choice might be CD-ROM, with circa 500 MB of capacity, but even then, for servers storing large amounts of data, the numbers of CD-ROMs required might become unmanageable. DAT tape has the largest capacity, measured in gigabytes. So, consider the physical quantity of media required to store the data you wish to back-up. In most instances some form of DAT tape will suffice, but CD-ROM does have certain advantages. For personal use, Zip drives with a capacity of up to 250 MB are an easy media to manage.

9.3.4 Reliability

If reliability of restoration is the overriding issue, then you should be considering CD-ROM or DAT tape. You should also examine the operational reliability and ease of use (in a crisis) of the restoration software that you are using.

9.3.5 Cost

This is the underlying issue to data backup. In financial terms, the cost of operating your backup and data recovery strategy, including cost of media, cost of storage, and cost of hardware, should not exceed the costs incurred by losing the data. In many cases, the cost of data backup will be capped by some degree of budgetary constraint with a need to demonstrate value for money. For obvious reasons, the majority of benefit/cost analysis shows that backing up data is more cost effective than data loss!

9.3.6 Safe storage of backup media

The storage of the backup media is in many instances a key part of the data recovery process. When the backup is made, the media should be stored in a location that is readily accessible in the event that restoration is required. The media should be accessible whatever the nature of the disaster that precipitates the need for restoration, and this may mean that in some instances the best storage location for backup media is offsite. This ensures the media can be accessed in the event of the workplace being closed or incapacitated.

A further advantage in keeping media offsite is that there is no need to worry about the protection of the backup media from the effects of disaster. To protect from fire, many system administrators use a fireproof storage device that prevents the media from burning. If you use one of these devices, then you must ensure that the heat within the storage container is kept sufficiently low that the media is protected not just from combustion, but also from the effects of moderate heating. Remember that heat will corrupt data on magnetic media. The storage media should also be stored in a location that offers sufficient protection from theft or unauthorized access. The backup data could have significant value in the wrong hands.

9.4 The importance of rehearsal!

Having carried out data backups of your system, you need to be sure that you can actually conduct a restoration of the data from the backup created. Often, the first time that network administrators find that something is amiss with their backup is when the restoration of data is actually required in a critical situation! Clearly, this is inappropriate. Alternatively, the backup is intact but in the heat of the moment, during a live restoration, things go wrong. You might discover that the backup device cannot be driven without certain files being loaded in the operating system, or some other oversight might arise whereby the backed-up data cannot be restored. Maybe the hardware required in order to read the media is just not present. The punchline is that you should not assume that you will be able to restore your data the first time you try, and you do not want to try to restore the system for the first time in a real live disaster recovery scenario. The key to getting live data restoration right first time is, of course, rehearsal. Rehearsals need not take place on live networks. Instead, trials could take place on lab systems configured to replicate the hardware in use as much as possible.

Arising out of the first few rehearsal processes should be a clear and repeatable procedure for data restoration. These procedures should then be captured and documented, with the names of those system administrators responsible for implementing the restoration. The procedures should then be referenced in all instances of data recovery being invoked. The procedures for data recovery will ultimately form part of your security policy. Like all procedures, these disaster recovery plans should be amended and updated when the need arises so that the procedures always reflect current practice. Arising out of these activities will be the confidence that restoration can be carried out when the need arises, right first time.

9.5 The worst case scenario

As we have seen, data restoration can be required for all manner of reasons; many cases of restoration being required on a single user basis, a crucial report has been accidentally deleted, for example. Altogether less likely is the need to restore data on an office-wide basis or, even less likely, on an organization-wide basis. Such instances are few and far between. But, disaster does strike some unfortunate organizations, often unexpectedly.

Imagine, for a moment, what is the worst case scenario your organization could be affected by, such that you would have to restore all data on the servers? Perhaps one of the servers crashing might necessitate complete data recovery. Perhaps a virus that has propagated throughout the network might necessitate restoration of the server to a clean state? Such instances are serious breaches of security that would require quick and rapid restoration of data. But what if, as well as having no data, you also had no server either, or worse still no office? Such a scenario would be 'worst case' indeed!

Such a worse case scenario might occur for various reasons, including:

- Weather damage, such as storms, flooding or damage by high winds.
- Building hazards, such as collapse, subsistence, or evacuation due to environment hazard.
- Criminal damage, such as vandalism, theft, or riots.
- Fire or explosion, or even the threat of a fire or explosion, leading to the evacuation and possible destruction of the premises.

Any of these events would halt the normal operation of your

organization. Certainly the network system would most likely be unavailable, either through destruction of the hardware or through forced evacuation of the building premises. In such a situation, how would you respond?

If you have no plan of mitigation in such an event, you are not alone. Many organizations find out the hard way that they cannot respond to disasters of this kind and actually end up going out of business the first time that a worse case scenario disaster strikes. Closure is not necessarily immediate, organizations find that in the time that follows disaster, they are simply unable to continue doing business following such massive disruption caused by the loss of working premises.

Even with alternative premises lined up, access to business information systems is still required at some point. The length of time which day-to-day operations can continue without access to network systems varies from organization to organization but for some organizations that are heavily dependent on information systems, even lack of availability of just a few minutes means that the organization will cease to operate. This means that just having a spare office to go to is of no help at all, what is needed is a plan for the continuation of the business using alternative network infrastructure, and the option of migration to, and subsequent continuity of the organization within, alternative premises.

In order to do all this, you will need to have access to the data necessary for the continued operation. New hardware might be relatively easy to come by, perhaps a new temporary office as well if a well-thought-out business continuity plan has been executed. But, the continuity plan will come to nothing if there is no data with which to replicate the information systems. In the event of the worst kind of disaster – complete destruction of working premises – some organizations are able to recover their business operations within four hours. This remarkable ability is due only to business continuity planning, rehearsal and readiness.

9.6 Business continuity

Organizations that are concerned about their ability to respond to worst case scenarios often plan for business continuity in the event of disaster. Data recovery is central to business continuity, but although the availability of backup is pivotal to the successful continuation of business, the business continuity plan includes far more than just the backup, safe storage, and subsequent restoration of data. The business continuity plan will include all actions necessary for the wholesale migration of operations to alternative premises, using alternative network hardware and software, in short a turnkey facility for business continuity. Included in most business continuity plans will be the following items.

9.6.1 Criteria for invoking the business continuity plan

Although in many instances of disaster striking, the need to invoke the business continuity plan will be quite clear, sometimes, the need will not be so cut and dried. In the event of a flood that affects only part of your building, just to what extent would the flood need to cause disruption before you invoke the plan? Like all instances of risk mitigation, there must be clear and unambiguous criteria that must occur or be met before the go ahead is given to action the plan. Moreover, the authority to action the plan must be ascertained as well. This should not be limited to one or two key people. Sod's law dictates that disaster will strike when they are all on holiday. There will be no time to call them and get the go ahead, so the ability to invoke the plan must be delegated to an appropriate number of key people throughout the organization.

9.6.2 Safe evacuation and co-ordination of personnel

When the business continuity plan is evoked in the event of disaster, there needs to be a clear and authoritative announcement that evacuation is to occur. All staff need to know where to congregate, and who to report to in the new location. The plan will not function if staff arrive at the congregation point in dribs and drabs, with no record kept of movements. Co-ordination is vital if the location and availability of staff are to be ascertained.

9.6.3 Roles and responsibilities

There will need to be a clear division of roles and responsibilities for implementing the migration process. In the event of disaster, situations evolve quickly and critical information needs to be reported to the right people. For this reason, everyone in the organization needs to know their own role within the plan, and the escalation chain up which to report certain events that may occur. Decision makers need to be prepared to make the appropriate decisions in a timely fashion when called for in the escalation process.

9.6.4 Preparation of equipment

Alternative equipment will need to be installed, tested and made live, all within as short a time as possible. Typically for many organizations, just a few hours of deployment time would be demanded, and this would include the setting up of new hardware, installation of operating system and data, configuration and installation of networking equipment, testing before and during the early stages of use.

9.6.5 Communications

Remember that computers and networking equipment are not the only communication systems required. Most organizations also require telephones and faxes. Arrangements will need to be made for call forwarding or re-routing in the event of migration to alternative premises.

9.7 Business continuity management

Many organizations decide on the basis of a cost benefit analysis to outsource their disaster recovery plans to a specialist third party. These specialist companies will undertake to provide a continuity of service cover on a 24 hour-a-day basis together with the provision of replacement hardware and software if required. In addition, an appropriate response time is assured. The reason business continuity specialists offer an attractive proposition is that the impact of disaster is high, and that by bringing in the experts, who are advising many similar organizations on business continuity, a great deal of collective experience can be brought to bear. There is nothing wrong with this approach of course. The confidence of an organization to recover from disaster is crucial to corporate well-being, as was demonstrated during preparations for the year 2000 changeover.

If instead you wish to manage business continuity plans in-house, and for many companies this is a preferred option, then there are several things to bear in mind:

- Ensure that data recovery procedures are rehearsed and work as planned. The recovery of data is critical to business continuity.

- Conduct a fair and proper risk assessment.
- Develop a strategy for continuing all crucial business operations, this may include sales, marketing, engineering, accounts, etc. There is more to running an organization than just the information systems.
- Implement procedures for continuing business in the event of migration to new premises, and also in the event of remaining in your office.
- Be very clear about what set of circumstances warrants invocation of the plan.
- Rehearsal is key! Hold a business continuity day, at least once a year, when the business continuity processes are rehearsed.
- Update the plan as often as operational circumstances dictate.

9.8 Review

- Data is a valuable asset, and mitigating actions need to be planned in the event of data loss.
- Data loss can occur for various reasons, including user and administrative error, software and hardware failure, viruses and attacks. Data loss can also occur due to accidents or disasters.
- Data recovery plans should include adequate measures for the backing up of data, and for the restoration of that data in the event of data loss. The procedure for restoration of data should be rehearsed!
- Attention should be paid to the safe transit, storage and retrieval of the backed-up data so that the availability of the data can be assured.
- Worst case scenario includes not just data loss, but complete loss of the network infrastructure and of the operational facilities.
- Appropriate disaster recovery plans need to be established and rehearsed in order that organizations can continue to operate in such events. Organizations that fail to do so will most likely suffer serious damage when disaster strikes if no such plans are in place.

9.9 To do

9.9.1 Document and rehearse recovery and continuity procedures

- Document best practice backup and recovery procedures for your organization.
- Establish what media should be used.

- Install appropriate storage facilities for restoration media with copies to be stored both on-and-off site.
- Rehearse the processes. Put your data recovery to the test, and challenge the IT team to restore a specific file or to rebuild a particular computer.
- Start to plan business continuity strategies for computer hardware and software, telephony systems, for the office premises and for staff.
- Document the procedures for business continuity.
- Rehearse and refine, on a regular basis, and if possible hold a business continuity day.

10

Firewalls

Firewalls are powerful tools, but they should never be used *instead* of other security measures. They should only be used in *addition* to such measures.
(*Practical Unix and Internet Security*, Garfinkel and Spafford)

Computer networks used to be self-contained, private LANs or WANs that enabled workstations and other hardware to communicate, often by using a proprietary protocol. Security was afforded in part by the physical isolation of the network from the world at large. Then, with the adoption of the Internet, networks became more heterogeneous as both the office LAN and the company WAN changed from using proprietary protocols to open systems TCP/IP. Organizations began to use the Internet for email, access to the Web, and also to join geographically remote offices and workers. But, as well as the clear benefits of greater integration to the outside world, connection to the Internet brings the added risks associated with interfacing a private (secure) network to a public network.

For various reasons – many cultural, some operational – a few organizations have reacted to that risk by preventing the widespread use of email or the Web. Other organizations have adopted a more measured approach of employee education coupled with security applications that place a semipermeable barrier between the organization's network and the Internet. The barrier generally takes the form of a firewall and other software that filters network traffic passing in and out of an organization's network.

Since the widespread increase in utilization of the Internet, firewalls are a de-facto mandatory requirement for organizations using the Internet. When configured correctly and used as part of the overall package of security measures a firewall can improve the security of an organization's Internet facing network. Firewalls can be used to control access to an organization's secure network, usually private, from an insecure network outside, usually the Internet, while at the same time providing relatively uninhibited access in the other direction.

A firewall is, though, just one part of an organization's overall security strategy, as documented in their security policy, and to this end, a firewall will not prevent security breaches per se, only reduce the possibility of external access occurring. The deployment of firewalls within an organization should be considered carefully as a single firewall placing a soft divide between the organization's intranet and the Internet will not in any way prevent unauthorized access by anyone from the inside. Often, therefore, large organizations may have several firewalls strategically deployed at various nodes within their network.

10.1 What exactly is a firewall?

A firewall is a device that filters network traffic, and can be:

- A single software application.
- A suite of configured applications.
- A hardware application.
- Any combination of the above that provides the ability to control the flow of network traffic between networks.

Data transiting through the firewall is filtered according to criteria specified within a firewall policy. At the most basic level of configuration, all traffic is either permitted to flow through the firewall or is denied, though this type of filtering would be of little practical use. For the firewall to be useful, network traffic through the firewall (Figure 10.1) is usually filtered according to the following criteria:

- Origin of the traffic, indicated by IP address or domain name.
- Destination of the traffic, specified by IP address or domain name.
- Destination port number, indicating the protocol being used by the application, for instance, FTP, HTTP, Telnet, etc. There are literally hundreds of different applications that can send traffic over TCP/IP.
- Time of the transaction.

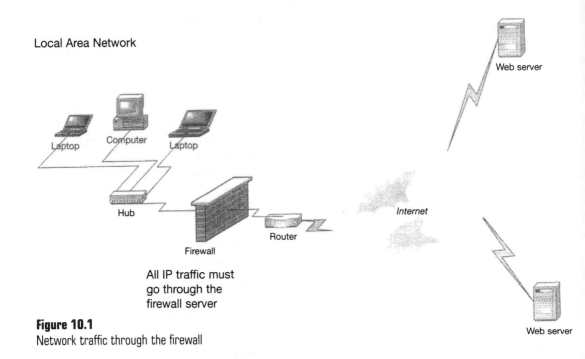

Figure 10.1
Network traffic through the firewall

10.1.1 Firewall policy

A firewall policy can be constructed around a basic policy of either *permit all* traffic to flow through the network unless specifically denied, or *deny all* traffic unless specifically permitted. Then, building upon the permit all or deny all policy, a rule base is constructed that provides exceptions to the underlying permit all or deny all policy. The policy should enable users of the organization's private network to access the Internet directly, but at the same time protecting the network from various types of threat, in particular:

- The threat of uncontrolled access to computers inside the private network, from the Internet.
- Uncontrolled Internet access by users within the private network, for example preventing access to various websites that are deemed to be unsuitable for corporate consumption, or permitting only email and Web traffic to be sent out, and nothing else.

10.2 Types of firewall

Although generally speaking all firewalls perform the same
basic function, that is to say they filter network traffic, there are
various methods by which the traffic filtering takes place. The
functionality of each different type of firewall varies depending
on which of the OSI network-levels the inspection of the
network traffic takes place (Figure 10.2). Different types of firewall employ inspection at one or more of these OSI levels. These
different types are defined below.

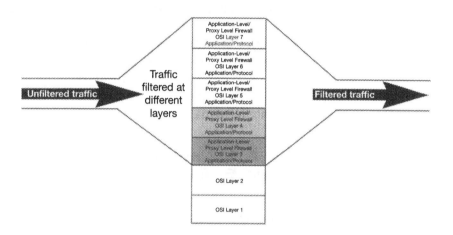

Figure 10.2
OSI network levels

10.2.1 Network level – OSI level 3

A network-level firewall will filter traffic according to characteristics of the IP packet being sent through the firewall. Criteria
usually include:

• Source and destination IP address.
• Source and destination port number.
• Protocol used.

Network-level firewalls are transparent to most users and are
therefore unintrusive and very fast. Some routers can be configured to act as network-level firewalls, which can be a useful and
low cost way of providing an initial barrier to incoming or
outgoing traffic across the public/private interface. Some implementations of network-level firewalls will also evaluate infor-

mation about the state of the connections passing through them and the actual content of the data.

10.2.2 Transport level – OSI level 4

Similar to the network-level firewall, but the transport-level firewall inspects traffic at the TCP level, corresponding to the transport layer of the OSI model. Inspection of the TCP part of the traffic enables filtering to be carried out on:

- The legitimacy of a session, for example whether or not a session has been initiated by a known source.

In common with network firewalls, transport-level firewalls are inexpensive. They have an advantage in that network traffic appears to have originated from the firewall's IP address, therefore masking the IP address of the true source from within the private network.

10.2.3 Application level, or proxy – OSI levels 5, 6, 7

Application-level firewalls are often referred to as proxy firewalls, which is a fair description of the application firewalls' behaviour. The application firewall provides protection by acting as an intermediary between the public and private networks. Say you wish to access a website, then you would send a request to the proxy. The proxy then sends the request out to the website on your behalf. The reply from the website is then sent to the proxy, which then sends the data back to you. In this way there is no direct network transaction occurring between you on the private network and the website on the Internet. The firewall inspects traffic by analysing data by:

- Protocol, such as FTP, HTTP, etc.
- Application

Unlike the firewalls based on lower OSI layers, application-level firewalls are not so fast, and are not transparent to users either, requiring some configuration on the user's workstation clients. Browsers that are using an application, or proxy-based, firewall need to have the relevant proxy settings entered into the appropriate configuration tab.

Also, a different proxy is required for each different protocol being inspected. This means that if an HTTP proxy is provided, by default users cannot use telnet or FTP through a firewall. This is good from a security point of view, but the overhead of having several proxies running on the same server are soon felt by latency and lag in the network.

There are advantages, though, inherent in application layer inspection, such as the ability to filter protocols and application requests by specific commands, thus the extent to which a particular service can be accessed through the firewall can be controlled. This is not possible at the lower level inspections. Also, user activity authentication can be inspected and logged.

10.2.4 Stateful inspection – OSI layers 3–7

In recent times, firewalls tend to include inspection on more than one layer, acting as a combination of the three firewall types discussed above, packet level, network level and application level. This hybrid inspection is called stateful inspection, or dynamic packet filtering. By combining the three inspection methods, the transparency of the network level firewall is retained. But examination of traffic content can also be carried out, as in an application type server, often by the use of more sophisticated techniques than a simple proxy. Stateful firewalls combine the best attributes of the three different types of firewall, giving inspection by all the criteria each individual firewall is able to use, but also providing speed and therefore low overhead to users. Most of the mainstream vendor firewalls are based on stateful inspection technology.

10.2.5 Some firewall concepts

Private network

The private network, sometimes referred to as the *clean side of the firewall*, is the part of the network that needs protecting. Usually this is an organization's internal LAN.

Public network

The public network, sometimes referred to as the *dirty side of the firewall*, is the part of the network over which no direct control can be exerted and is deemed to be publicly available. Usually, the public network is the Internet.

Choke point

The concept of a choke point is crucial to the architectural design of the firewall network. In order for a firewall to provide complete protection to the private network, all network traffic in transit between the public and private networks must pass through a single point, the choke point. Any traffic transiting between the two networks, and not passing through the choke point represents a leak in the firewall. Modems are the most common leaks, enabling TCP/IP to pass from private to public network without inspection by the firewall. The choke point between the two networks is usually the firewall host or gateway.

Bastion host

The bastion host is the term applied to the computer on which the firewall software is installed, and as such has a critical role in the firewall implementation. Usually, the bastion host has stringent security measures applied. Modifications are made to the standard operating system installation, usually in the form of stripped down services and usability. A Windows NT bastion host might have no need for the SMB server and workstation services, for instance. These two services could provide an easy means of determining the operating system being used on the host, and could be used to crash the bastion host by exploiting vulnerabilities, and therefore causing denial of service.

Gateway

The gateway is the network device that receives and transmits network traffic from a private to public network and back again. A dual-homed gateway (Figure 10.3) is a computer that has two network interface cards installed. One of the cards belongs to the private network, the other to the public network. As such, the dual-homed gateway straddles two separate networks and passes network traffic back and forth in proxy fashion. All incoming traffic terminates at the incoming network device on the public network and is then passed to the other interface card, which belongs to the secure network, if the criteria for allowing traffic to flow through the firewall are satisfied. The dual-homed gateway therefore has two IP addresses. A multi-homed gateway is the same in concept as a dual-homed gateway, but with multiple network interface cards instead of just two cards.

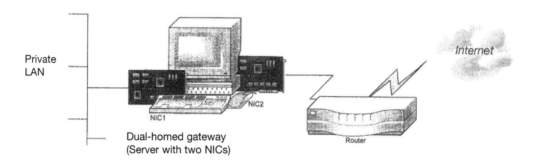

Private
LAN

NIC1

NIC2

Dual-homed gateway
(Server with two NICs)

Internet

Router

Figure 10.3
The dual-homed gateway

Router screening

Most contemporary routers have some capacity to restrict
network traffic, usually by matching source domain names or IP
addresses to a list of prohibited names. Router screening is fast,
but often lacks the logging abilities that come with more
complex firewall software. Screening routers operate at the
network-level and therefore make their decisions on the basis of
the information contained in the IP traffic.

DMZ

DMZ stands for demilitarized zone. This is the zone around the
firewall where public facing computers are situated. Instances
of such computers might include Web servers. Mail servers on
the other hand are usually kept behind the firewall on the
private side. In practice the DMZ is usually a server connected
between the public network and the firewall.

A typical live deployment

In this instance, the positions of the mail server and the Web
server in Figure 10.4 are shown relative to the firewall and the
DMZ.

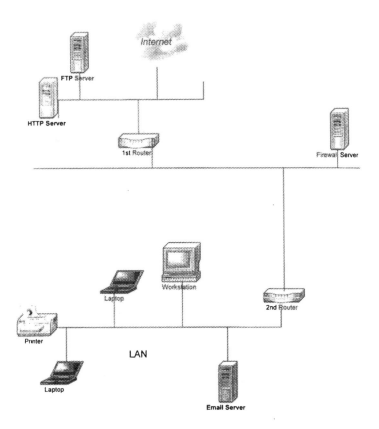

Figure 10.4
A typical deployment

10.3 Limitations to firewalls

As with any technical solution, a firewall is not a fit and forget solution to a security problem. Initially, the firewall must be installed and configured correctly, and the system administrator must also ensure that there are no architectural problems with the underlying network infrastructure. Then, the firewall will need continual maintenance and updating. Finally, users must be educated about the firewall's functionality and operational constraints so that they understand why they are not able to perform certain functions or perhaps visit certain websites.

Despite a firewall being installed within an organization's network, there are still certain types of risk that remain a threat to the network security, and that the firewall will be able to play no part in addressing. Bear in mind that the firewall can only control threats contained in network traffic that actually flows through the choke point. For this reason, the firewall will not prevent:

- Users connecting modems to their computers in order to bypass the firewall and gain Internet access.

- Users on the inside from attempting to gain unauthorized access to internal servers, unless those servers are protected by a dedicated internal firewall of their own.
- A firewall can only protect a network that has been correctly configured and works as expected.

On occasions the firewall will fail to protect the network from breaches. Indeed, there have been some reported instances where a firewall has been cracked open and the private network revealed and accessed. A firewall is, after all, an application that needs to be installed correctly, and then maintained, and perhaps updated with software patches. If the firewall is not installed or maintained correctly, then problems may occur. Some of the other reasons why firewalls fail to live up to expectation are:

- The entire security policy rests on the firewall, so that other security measures like password control and secure configuration of workstations and servers are not attended to. The result is an insecure network with a protected perimeter that will continue to be subjected to security breaches caused by inside users.
- The firewall is seen as a fit and forget solution, whereby the firewall is left in a state of gradual disrepair. New vulnerabilities are being discovered continually, and new protocols are being developed and deployed. A firewall that is not maintained and adjusted in line with changes in operational circumstances will soon become outmoded. At the very worst, vulnerabilities in the firewall will be discovered and then used against the installation.
- The firewall is let down by a faulty network installation, such as there being an uncontrolled access point into the private network, or there being incorrectly set-up routing, which could allow the choke point and gateway to be bypassed.

10.4 Do you need a firewall?

This is the $64 000 question that many organizations ask themselves when starting to use the Internet. Like all security measures, the answer to this question must be weighed up in terms of the potential cost of a security breach, of the type that a firewall can prevent from occurring, versus the one-off cost of implementation and the added ongoing cost of maintaining a firewall.

Of course, the best way to secure a network from the outside world is to remove the connection between the private network and the Internet, thus completely isolating the private network. After all, an isolated network is the most secure network of all! So, perhaps the real question that should be asked is not do you need a firewall but are the risks incurred in connecting your organization's network directly to the Internet acceptable to your organization, when balanced against the need to use the Internet? For many organizations, the benefits of using the Internet far outweigh the risks, and so a firewall is used as the best form of protection available in such situations.

However, a minority of organizations continue to keep some or all of their networks physically isolated from the Internet, because they are working with highly sensitive information, such as financial data, or are conducting work on behalf of the Government. In the event of security being compromised by some third party outside of the organization, the consequences could be grave; for instance, the organization might suffer serious damage to the extent that continued operations are impossible, or there may be a serious threat to national security. Even if a firewall is used, and the likelihood of breaches is much reduced, the impact of a breach would be too high to countenance. For those organizations, a firewall would simply not provide the 100 per cent assurance of protection from outside intrusion required.

If you have a modem or ISDN dialup connection, then there is a case to be made for not using a firewall. The risk of unauthorized access must be balanced with the temporary nature of the connection and the fact that the IP address of the modem or ISDN device will most likely be dynamically assigned, and will probably be different each time the device is used. If you use fixed access then you should probably get a firewall.

10.5 Review

- A firewall is a software or hardware application or suite of applications that provides the ability to control the flow of network traffic according to various criteria, including origin and destination IP addresses, destination port and time of transaction.
- Firewall policies are based on a default deny or default permit policy.
- The question to ask is not 'do we need a firewall?' but 'do we need a connection to an insecure network such as the Internet?'
- Firewalls can filter network traffic at various levels of the OSI seven layer model.

- There are limitations to firewalls, in that they cannot prevent misuse of the network, for instance through the connection of modems to desktop computers, nor can they work as expected if the network has been configured incorrectly.
- The firewall is not a 'fit and forget' solution that is an alternative to network security policy. The role of the firewall is to support the enforcement of the policy.

10.6 To do

10.6.1 Evaluate your firewall requirements

- Be clear of the benefits and costs of being connected to the Internet.
- Document the access points from your network to the Internet.
- Uninstall modems that are connected to user's workstations.
- Speak to vendors, download and evaluate their products using your test lab.
- Speak to your IT team and establish whether there is enough knowledge in-house to build a firewall or to manage the installation of a firewall by a third party or vendor.
- Identify the choke points where a firewall should be installed. Plan any changes that may be required to the existing network.
- If you plan to scan content, such as virus scanning, then check that your firewall is compatible with the content scanning software you are considering.
- Ensure that the firewall bastion host has a suitably stripped down operating system installed with absolutely no add-ons or extras. The firewall should not be compromised as a result of vulnerabilities within the host operating system.

11

Content security

Subject: Here you have, ;o)
Attachment: AnnaKournikova.jpg.vbs
Message: Hi: Check This!

With a firewall in place, many organizations have secured the interface between their private networks and the Internet. They have also taken great steps to ensure the security of their operating systems and servers. Yet there is still potential for security breaches to arise. In fact, some of the more widespread security incidents, which affected not just a single organization but the entire Internet, have been content security breaches. Often, in these widespread instances, the threat arises from email viruses.

In the past, viruses sent by email used to be nothing more than a myth. Those who used email during the early 1990s will recall receiving so-called virus alerts sent by well-meaning colleagues warning them not to open any email messages containing the subject 'Penpals wanted', for instance. Being concerned, and wanting to help others, many people dutifully forwarded these messages onto their friends, colleagues, and family, and kept an eye out for the said email messages. Of course, the whole thing was a spoof. The whole point of the email was to cause disruption and concern in much the same way as a chain letter, you receive the email and forward the contents to all of the people you know, and so the email message perpetuates.

Now, though, the situation regarding virus propagation by email is very different, as was illustrated most dramatically by the Melissa virus. This is because email client applications such as Microsoft Outlook are able to interpret and execute the attachment containing programming or scripting code. The same scripting code can be used to write viruses that can then be included in email messages. The Melissa virus first appeared in the news group alt.sex and, from there, quickly spread by email. The virus used Microsoft Outlook to infect a host computer, hence corporate users of the Microsoft Office suite were most affected. Within hours, Microsoft, NASA, and government organizations were hit and were forced to take their computers down. The Melissa virus caused several security breaches.

Such content security breaches can arise because, secure though the private network perimeter is, network traffic that passes the various inspection criteria is still permitted to pass through. The assumption is that because a network service is being controlled, i.e. authorized and permitted to pass through any firewall, the service poses no threat. This is far from the truth. Although these services are considered safe or acceptable to use, a security threat is present from within the content of the network traffic, which often passes through the firewall uncontrolled. Although the data passes all the inspection tests, the data content has not been tested. In other words, do we know whether or not the email contains a virus? These content threats can be categorized into four main areas.

11.1 Programming and scripting languages

Scripting languages are used commonly within HTML documents to provide enhanced interaction of Web pages. In the context of email, clients can read email messages and execute scripting and programming attachments automatically, for instance Microsoft email clients have the facility to execute ActiveX components that are sent by email attachment. This means that malicious code can be written in the scripting language, enclosed with an email, and then executed on the target computer. A worrying and hypothetical scenario would be if someone wrote a script to send the contents of your recently saved documents to a third party. There are four scripting languages used to generate active content, these are reviewed below.

11.1.1 JavaScript

JavaScript was developed by Netscape Corporation, at around the same time as the development of the browser Netscape

Navigator 2. Not to be confused with Java, which is something very different, JavaScript is a scripting language in which the commands are sent to the client and then executed without compilation. This mode of operation should be compared to programs written in programming languages, such as C or C++, which need to be compiled prior to execution.

JavaScripts can be included within HTML documents, and the client browser interprets the script commands as the document downloads, in order to provide interactivity within Web pages. Examples of such interactivity include some renditions of the popular rollover animated buttons on Web pages, the generation of pop-up child windows within the Web browser, or to check completed Web forms for syntax errors.

JavaScript can also be included within email, which is then interpreted by email clients such as Netscape Messenger. Although JavaScript is supposed to be portable between different browser client applications, in practice there will be slight differences between the results obtained from Netscape Navigator and Internet Explorer when some scripts are interpreted.

As a scripting language, JavaScript has undergone some revisions. Part of the refinement and updating of the language was the removal of a great many of the security loopholes that were found to exist. Now, many of the security issues that arise with JavaScript are more to do with privacy concerns, and thus impact upon private individuals perhaps more so than organizations. Moreover, the security holes more often than not were due to the implementation of the JavaScript interpreter contained within the browser, i.e. they were software bugs in the interpreter. Some *past* security concerns were:

- Ability to read arbitrary files on the client computer due to bugs in the JavaScript interpreter within the Web client.
- Remote websites could read URLs from the browser cache, allowing a list of sites recently visited by the user to be compiled.
- JavaScript could be used to trick the user into uploading files to a third party machine on the Internet. Although the user must click a button in order to initiate the transfer, the button can easily be made to masquerade as something else. Nor is there any indication that a file transfer has occurred before or after the event.
- A JavaScript could be written in order to obtain directory listings of the user's local hard disk and any network shares. This represented a serious security risk since mapping an organ-

ization's network architecture is a great advantage for devising a way to break in.

Although these are old and well-known bugs, they illustrate the extent to which active content could cause breaches of security. New bugs are discovered all the time. For this reason, many organizations prefer not to permit JavaScript to be used within their secure network. One such organization, an asset management company, had to write two versions of the company website after realizing that the JavaScript driven website that had just been rolled out was not readable by employees in the company premises. Only organizations where security is a paramount concern should consider prohibiting JavaScript.

11.1.2 Java

Java is altogether something rather different to JavaScript. Developed by Sun Microsystems, Java is a programming language designed to be portable, able to run on varied operating systems, and to be used over distributed networks such as the Internet. Java is similar to C++, and as such is object oriented. The story goes that Java was first designed to be run on electrical appliances such as washing machines, but these days Java is used to provide interactivity within Web documents or to deploy small applications, called applets, over the Web.

The main advantage of Java is the portability of the language. Java programs are compiled into code that can be run anywhere on a client that has a Java virtual machine. The role of the virtual machine is to act as an interpreter to the Java, enabling the portable code to run on specific hardware and operating system combinations. Both Netscape Communicator and Internet Explorer have Java virtual machines that can be used to execute Java applets.

There are several controls contained within Java code and within the Virtual Machine implementation that help prevent secure breaches occurring. Java execution is controlled by a security manager which does not normally allow applets to gain uncontrolled access to the client computer and Java applets are usually restricted to only being able to read and write to a user defined working directory. Also, an applet can only make a connection back to the originating server. Finally, the security manager allows Java applets to read and write to the network, read and write to the local disk, but not both. Some Java Virtual Machines provide additional barriers, for instance Netscape

Communicator disables all local file manipulation by Java applets.

Of course, any application that is able to send and receive data from a local client to a remote server poses a potential threat to network security. Some instances of *past* vulnerabilities arising from Java use were:

- Vulnerabilities to memory buffer overflow in virtual machines could cause the host computer to crash.
- Denial of service attacks could be launched by utilizing an applet's tendency to overload the local client's computer memory and CPU. This tendency could be exploited maliciously to bring down a user's computer.
- Early versions of Netscape Navigator contained vulnerabilities that could be exploited to enable applets to contact arbitrary hosts on the Internet.

Most of the vulnerabilities have been fixed in subsequent versions of Java and in the later releases of the virtual machines which interpret the Java code.

11.1.3 VBScript

VBScript is a scripting language developed by Microsoft. The script language is a subset of Microsoft's Visual Basic programming language and offers similar functionality to JavaScript. In contrast to the open adoption of JavaScript, however, VBScript is used with Internet Explorer only. Netscape does not support VBScript.

Although VBScript does not offer file access or access to the operating system, the risks associated with VBScript are second to none where active content is concerned. All the big virus outbreaks that have happened of late – the Kournikova, Melissa and I Love You viruses spring to mind – are derived from exploiting the VBScript capabilities of Microsoft client applications. In each of these incidents, the virus was written using VBScript, which was in turn interpreted by the email client, usually Microsoft Outlook.

Case Study – Anyone for tennis?

One high profile incident that illustrates the way that VBScript can be used to spread viruses was the Kournikova virus that affected many of those organizations that use Microsoft Outlook. The virus is a VBScript that spread via email. The main impact of the virus was a denial of service caused by flooding of email servers and of network capacity. When executed, the virus took various actions.

Copies of the virus were sent to all entries in each of the Outlook address books. The messages sent had a subject line stating 'Here you have, ;o)' and the message said 'Hi: Check This!', referring to the attachment 'AnnaKournikova.jpg.vbs'. Now, here is the crux of the virus. By default, Windows operating systems hide the file suffix from the user, so the VBScript appeared to be a JPEG file, not a script file. Also, because the recipient was in another's address book, the chances are that these two users are acquaintances and the file would not appear to be from an unknown source.

On the face of things, the virus appears harmless. You receive an email, and then email is sent out again to further recipients. But, the types of organizations that use Outlook tend to be large companies, with tens of thousands of users. As the virus percolates rapidly through the organization, perhaps picking up on company-wide email distribution lists, the capacity of the network and of the mail server is soon met. Many companies that were affected found that they were without services for a few hours or so. To an individual, this would be a minor inconvenience, to a large company a major headache.

To protect against the threats posed by VBScript in this regard, the easy way is to prevent VBScripts from entering your secure network, through content filtering, or disable the VBScript from being interpreted by reconfiguring the client application. The harder way, if you want the benefits of VBScript, is to ensure that you patch and update software as soon as new releases become available, accepting that without other controls in place you may be at significant risk of virus infection.

11.1.4 ActiveX

ActiveX is another content technology developed by Microsoft, but this time with some similarities to Java. Like Java, ActiveX is distributed over the Internet, usually within a Web page, in the form of an ActiveX control. Only Internet Explorer, however, supports ActiveX controls. A key distinction from Java is that ActiveX controls are distributed as executable binaries, and so must be compiled for each target machine and operating system. Thus, ActiveX is not portable in the way that Java is.

Security is a concern in that there are no restrictions on what an ActiveX control can do. The user of an ActiveX control is instead expected to view the credentials of a control, containing a digital stamp of the author, and choose whether or not to allow the control to be executed. The author is in effect claiming that the ActiveX control will be free of harmful effects. But a malicious user is not likely to claim otherwise! Moreover, users need to be aware of exactly what they are doing when they download and use ActiveX controls. Users are able to run controls from untrusted sources if they wish, and the browser presents a dialog box warning the user that this action may not be safe. Users can elect to abort the download, or may continue the download and take their chances.

Case Study – Exploder

To illustrate the dangers of ActiveX, a software developer called Fred McLain published an ActiveX control named Exploder. This control, which was signed and certified, performs a clean shutdown of any Windows 95 machine on which the ActiveX control is executed. The shutdown occurs automatically, just after the user has viewed a Web page containing the Exploder ActiveX control when using Microsoft Internet Explorer.

After learning about Exploder, the certifying authorities revoked McLain's certified digital signature, claiming that he had violated the agreement made when the certification was issued. Therefore, if you are running a newer version of Internet Explorer, you will see a message that Exploder's software certificate is invalid.

While Exploder does not cause any data loss, a less friendly control might reformat the user's hard disk or plant a virus or Trojan. In fact, a series of highly malicious ActiveX controls have been created and distributed by the Chaos Computer Club of Hamburg, Germany. They are unsigned controls, meaning that with its default settings in place, Internet Explorer will warn the user that they are not to be trusted. However, naive users who have changed Internet Explorer's restrictions on active content to 'Low Security', or who agree to download and execute the controls despite the warnings, are vulnerable to attack by this means.

ActiveX should not be used in a secure environment. There is an unacceptable degree of onus put on the user to make an informed decision, often in circumstances where they are likely to just wish to continue downloading the Web page they are viewing.

11.2 Text content

Not all content security threats have to be based around new and more complicated technology. Some threats to security can arise out of the text that is contained within an email or within an attached document. The threat from text content then takes the form of action or damage to an organization's position that might occur if the text was disclosed to a wider audience than was intended within the organization, made public, or sent to an unauthorized third party. The types of threat that can arise fall into the following main categories. While the impact can in some cases be large, there are ways in which the threat can be reduced, through user education and through text content scanning tools.

11.2.1 Offensive language

There is legislation in the UK, and also in the US, that makes the use of specific types of language an offence in certain circumstances. Examples of such language might be:

- Language that causes racial offence.
- Language that incites hatred or violence.
- Language that is prejudicial to gender.
- Language that is libellous.

Content that falls foul of these criteria would cause great damage to an organization when included within an email message, either to the originating or recipient organization.

11.2.2 Confidential material

This is a more serious threat than the previous, in that often the damage is not noticed, and can be part of an ongoing undermining of an organization's position. Most organizations have some information that they would rather not be in the public domain. This might include information that is financially sensitive, or might include information regarding a company's strategic plans for the future. Company insiders, acting for a competitor or predator, are not uncommon, and can cause tremendous damage.

Ask yourself now, what is preventing you from sending company confidential material to the outside world using email? In many cases, the answer would be very little apart from trust.

11.3 Images and multimedia

When first used, email messages contained ASCII text only. Then the MIME standard was adopted, which enables the attachment of additional files to the main email message. Now, emails can be sent with JPEG or GIF image files or with multimedia files attached to the message text. These sort of files pose various risks, on occasions due to their large size in comparison to a plain text email, or due to their inappropriate content.

11.3.1 File size

Regardless of the actual content of attached files, image files tend to be fairly large, of the order of KB, and multimedia files can be quite large, of the order of MB. When combined with the usual pattern of distribution, these relatively large file sizes can cause the resources of some email servers and networks to be stretched. Sometimes, these multimedia files are attached to email messages sent between friends and colleagues, distributed in the same widespread fashion as the joke emails. This means in practice that the same file attachment is sent to most people in an organization, consuming file storage space and also consuming some network bandwidth. On occasions single file attachments, even if sent for business purposes, may be sufficiently large to cause a server or network to slow down temporarily.

11.3.2 Inappropriate content

As well as size, there is the actual content of the multimedia being sent by email. Let's be realistic, no one is going to be sending pictures of their family holiday to their friends or colleagues; the pictures are usually rather more salacious. In recent times, organizations are taking an increasingly draconian line on the distribution of indecent pictures by email. Often, when incidents come to light in businesses, all employees involved will be dismissed or disciplined. Organizations are becoming increasingly aware of the threats arising from the potential for litigation arising from the distribution of indecent pictures, and are no longer willing to tolerate or downplay such actions. On some occasions, the problem is so rife that dismissal of everyone involved would be unfeasible and this is the only reason some people keep their jobs when caught.

Organizations should take action to prevent the distribution of such material in order to avoid any accusation of sexual harassment or publication of pornography. As case law evolves, and the judiciary become more aware of the circumstances and controls that are available, then inaction might be seen to be a contributory cause to the offence. Certainly, organizations would not wish to be seen in the public domain to be tolerating pornography in the workplace.

11.4 Protection measures

Content threats to network security are many and varied. For this reason, a strategic and high-level approach to protection against content security threats is required. Protection against content security threats should be placed at three specific locations:

- The interface between the Internet and the secure network, using content scanning software including scanning for viruses.
- At the server, through installation of virus detection software.
- At the workstation, through installation of virus detection software and the appropriate configuration of client software.

Let's review these options, and how they can be deployed at each particular location.

11.4.1 Virus scanning software

Virus scanning software is perhaps the oldest of the content security protection measures available. Although commonly deployed on desktop workstations, virus scanners are also available that can scan network traffic at the point of ingress to the secure network. As such they are often closely associated with firewalls and can be configured to occupy the same physical server and to work in co-operation with the firewall. Whatever virus scanner you use, you should remember the cardinal rule:

- Virus scanners are only as good as the latest update.

In other words, for a virus scanner to be effective, the criteria against which files or content is scanned must be updated regularly and frequently. This is because, quite simply, new viruses and variants of existing viruses are being developed all the time. One blue chip organization had a policy of updating their laptop virus detection software 'every six months or so' – woefully inadequate!

Virus scanners work by executing various checks on file structure, disk storage space and memory. File data is compared to characteristics of known viruses, or by the use of various descriptions of the data structures that could in theory be encountered within a virus. Polymorphic viruses, which change their data structure, can therefore be detected.

Scanners can work in various ways when installed, either working on demand, to scan a whole hard drive or floppy disk drive, or working in real time whereby each file that is opened is scanned prior to use. Real time scanning is more effective, as viruses can be detected as soon as they are apparent on a computer, but also takes valuable resources and can slow down the execution and use of applications.

As well as scanning for the presence of recognized code, some scanners can scan for changes to existing files. These compare the state of files at installation to the state they are in when the scanner is later invoked. Any difference in a file's state could suggest that the file has been modified, perhaps by the action of a virus. A drawback is that such scanners cannot work with new files where there is no assurity of the file being uncorrupted, unless a trusted signature of the file's state is also sent.

Virus scanners can be deployed in one of three locations:

- At the interface between the Internet and the secure network.
- On each client or server computer.

Often there is some uncertainty as to where the virus software should be installed. The correct question to ask first of all is, what are the ways in which virus infected files could enter the secure network?

- If you are connected to the Internet, then you should install a virus scanner in between the point of entry into your secure network, and any other hardware such as servers or clients.
- Then, if you permit floppy disks or CD-ROMs to be used for file storage or transfer, you should also install virus software on those computers that have such facilities if you believe the risk from viruses to be significant. All the evidence would suggest that this is the case.
- Laptops should be seen as a particularly high risk in this regard, as floppy disks are often used to transfer data to and from the laptop, particularly when out of the office. All laptops should have adequate and updated virus protection

software installed, the urgency being perhaps more apparent than with desktop computers.

11.4.2 Text scanning

Text scanning techniques, whereby the text content of mail and of attached documents can be read, can be deployed in order to prevent email messages being sent that contain inappropriate language or confidential material. Scanning text is fairly straightforward, email is sent as ASCII text in transit, and most documents also contain their text in a machine legible format, within the various formatting control characters. The hard part is enabling the software to judge whether or not a breach has taken place.

Scanning for particular words is easy. A dictionary of forbidden words can be compiled and the messages scanned to see whether any of these words are present. Thus, profanities and derogatory words can be easily picked up and the email or attachment refused transit. In the same way, words that might imply that the email or attached documents contain sensitive information, such as 'confidential', 'top', or 'secret', can be included in the dictionary to flag up documents that might not be suitable for sending beyond the confines of the organization. This type of analysis can at times prove to be a little simplistic, as words like 'pussy' can crop up in entirely acceptable contexts. Most products therefore use more advanced methods of text analysis which account for context, phrases and the proximity of the words or expressions.

11.4.3 Attachment scanning

An extrapolation of the principle of text scanning is to scan file attachments within email for other criteria. For example:

- File extension, so as to prevent certain file types from being sent to and from the organization in the form of email attachments. Organizations might choose to prevent image files from being attached to emails, to help prevent the circulation of indecent or inappropriate images.
- File size, so as to prevent very large files from entering the network and causing the slowing down of the email server or of the network activity.
- Unknown data formats, in order to prevent content being disguised before being sent out of the organization.

Messages that are filtered out of the network traffic by falling foul of one of the criteria selected can be either deleted, returned to sender, or stored in a holding area where the message may be held for further examination and action.

11.4.4 Active content and macro filtering and stripping

We have already seen how one of the greatest threats to secure networks lies in the active content that is sent with emails and sometimes embedded within HTML documents. The good news is that scripts and other active content such as Java applets and ActiveX controls can be stripped out of network traffic as they pass into your network. The content stripping is usually done just after network traffic enters the secure network through the firewall, and removes any potentially harmful content that is judged to be of risk to the network.

Email messages or Web documents are disassembled, if necessary, scanned and the prohibited content removed. Then the message or document is reassembled and forwarded to the intended destination. The side effect of this is that some mail messages or Web pages that rely upon active content will no longer work as intended by the sender.

11.4.5 URL blocking

Content downloaded from the Web can be filtered on the basis of the URL, or Web address, from where the content originates. This means that certain websites can effectively be placed out of bounds on a permanent or time restricted basis, so employees can be denied access to the following:

- Adult websites.
- Employment agency websites.
- Websites related to popular television programmes.
- The various browser-based email sites, such as hotmail, could also be barred during working hours. Indeed, these websites present specific risks to security, because they permit content to be sent via email to another destination, but at the same time bypassing the normal route for checking email, using instead http. Some organizations that employ email content scanning may overlook this hole, and fail to realize that sending uncontrolled email is still possible.

11.4.6 Client configuration

As well as the various software solutions outlined above, there are other steps that should be taken to minimize the risk from content security. Proper configuration of the various client applications used to read email and browse the Web is one aspect to controlling content that is often overlooked. *Proper configuration should also be accompanied by regular and appropriate updating of the application, using patches and service releases.*

Web clients

Both Internet Explorer and Netscape Communicator have a high degree of configuration control, so that the various active content interpreters can be either enabled or disabled.

In a highly secure network all JavaScript, Java, ActiveX, and VBScript facilities should be disabled, therefore preventing these programs from running on your client computers. To a lesser or greater degree, all of these programming languages have security holes that enable a malicious programmer to breach security.

Malicious programs written in Java, JavaScript or ActiveX are often designed to exploit browser weaknesses. Browsers contain bugs and exploitation of these bugs by programming code can cause the browser to crash, leaving the browser in a state where arbitrary remote code can be executed on your computers. Be aware of the fact that disabling these components will prevent some websites from functioning correctly.

For networks where security is not required to be so high, you may consider permitting Java and perhaps even JavaScript. Think carefully and weigh up the security risks before permitting VBScript and ActiveX to be enabled in browsers.

Email clients

Generally speaking, the same rules of thumb apply to email client applications as they do to Web browsers.

- Pay particular regard to the use of VBScripts within email clients, several recent viruses have been composed from VBScript.
- Disable the automatic execution of applications or file attachments that come with email.

11.5 Review

- Content security threats arise from the content contained within the application layer of network traffic.
- Instances of content threats include viruses, Trojans, active content, text content, and inappropriate content.
- The threat from viruses is well appreciated, and can be managed using appropriate virus scanning software.
- The threat from active scripting is appreciated less so; the best way of reducing the threat is to prevent the use of VBScript and ActiveX within HTML documents or email attachments.
- Text content poses significant threats as confidential or offensive content can be sent from the secure network unimpeded without appropriate content scanning.
- Images and multimedia content can pose a threat due to the file size or the nature of the content.
- Content scanning tools can be deployed at the network's interface with the external Internet.
- Web URLs can be blocked using the appropriate software.
- Web clients and email clients should be configured with security in mind, in particular active content should be disabled as should the automatic execution of file attachments.

11.6 To do

11.6.1 Start to pay attention to content

- Install a virus scanning application at each potential point of ingress into the secure network. Normally this is the interface with the Internet, and at the workstation and server due to floppy disks and CD-ROMs being used.
- Disable the use of VBScripts and Active X. Consider whether you should permit the use of JavaScript and Java.
- Consider whether to install additional scanning software to scan incoming emails for various types of content risks.
- Decide whether you are going to block URLs of various websites. If so, evaluate and procure software that can block URLs.
- Establish, with input from personnel, what type of content might breach the rules of acceptable use.
- Discourage users from automatically opening up attachments they are not expecting or do not recognize.
- Enable window operating systems to display full file names,

including the file suffix. Many viruses are misleadingly named virus.jpg.vbs, which then becomes virus.jpg when file name suffixes are hidden.

Security policy

Security should be driven by business need. Controls should be
designed to make best use of the facilities provided by technology,
but must also cover the people and the processes that make the
technology work.

(KPMG *Information Security Survey 2000*)

12.1 Introduction

This is where the hard work begins! At this stage you have probably already addressed some of the problem areas you have
identified within your organization, and are now ready to back
up your actions with security policy. This final chapter gives
you a way forward for putting in place a security policy that, as
part of your organization's procedures, will involve and apply
to everyone in your organization. The justification for a security
policy is reviewed, together with a review of the arguments in
favour of policy implementation required if the support of the
board of directors is to be obtained. This support is essential to
have, as without board support the security policy will carry no
weight. Then, the planning processes required to implement a
security policy are discussed together with the various ways in
which the policy can be drafted and implemented.

12.2 The need for a security policy

A security policy is needed to reconcile together all the working
practices and procedures within an organization, which exist

around information systems, and to place these practices and procedures on a formal footing. A well-constructed security policy takes the technical, and often to most people remote, issues of information security and places them in a context whereby they can be readily understood and appreciated, and therefore followed and adhered to.

If you are still in any doubt as to the value of network security and of a security policy, then consider the utilization of networked information systems within your organization. Payroll, accounts, sales, marketing, research and development, human resources, are all facilitated by the use of networked information systems. Networked information systems are depended upon by the entire organization. There is probably no business process in your organization that is untouched by information systems. There can therefore be no argument against implementing a security policy to safeguard the continued well-being of networked information systems, and ensure that all the business processes are supported without interruption. Remember, network security is about maintaining the availability, integrity and confidentiality of information.

12.3 Aims and purposes of a security policy

Generally speaking, a security policy will be used to document the various procedures and guidance for the secure configuration, management and use of the networked information systems; however, implementation of a security policy will also have other specific aims and purposes in mind. Some of these aims and purposes are itemized below, but more than likely you will have additional aims and purposes particular to your organization and operational circumstances.

12.3.1 Definition of the problem domain

A security policy will define, delineate and clarify just what network and computer security means in the context of your organization's operational requirements. In the absence of a security policy, nobody has a clear understanding of how network security affects them. Guidance is therefore received from a variety of not so well-informed sources, and misinformation and half-truths become rife. This is not a good environment for security. Only when the issues are clarified will they be appreciated and understood by the majority of the user community.

12.3.2 Definition of responsibility

Of course, at a basic level, everyone in the organization is responsible for security. There will be various individuals, however, who will carry a greater share of that responsibility than most. These individuals, the system administrator, the head of information services, the appropriate director responsible, etc., need to be included by role and name within the policy. With the exception of the system administrator, though, these people will probably not be responsible for the daily implementation of policy. Those who are implementing the policy will most likely be help desk and support staff, who need to be listed by role so that they and the users are aware of their importance in ensuring that the security policy is maintained.

12.3.3 Education

There are a great many people who are quite simply computer illiterate, sometimes through no fault of their own, sometimes because of their own choice. Whatever the reason, those users are barely equipped to use their computers in a productive fashion. This situation poses a huge security risk. Any activity that can increase a user's computer literacy will reduce that security risk. When written in the correct way – clear, helpful and approachable – the security policy can have an added educational value that can raise users' general awareness of information systems so that fewer breaches due to user error or ignorance occur. Remember that many security breaches occur due to user error. By educating users, that proportion of breaches can surely be reduced.

12.3.4 To increase security and reduce breaches

Of course the main aim of the security policy should be to increase the levels of security and therefore reduce the number and impact of security breaches occurring.

12.4 Applicability

To whom should the policy apply? The answer is easy. The security policy should apply to everyone, and as far as possible without exception. Of course this can be a problem in some cases. Who, for instance, is going to delete the managing director's unauthorized software, or remove the CEO's modem?

As a security administrator, the challenge is to find a way of ensuring no one slips through the net. One of the best ways of getting total applicability to all staff, including senior staff, is to involve the board at all stages in the drafting and implementation of the policy. The extent of their involvement will naturally depend upon their degree of hands-on interest, though you should encourage their participation at all times.

The security policy must also be constructed so that no impediment is placed in anyone's way, preventing them from doing their work. Any issues that are likely to arise, such as the installation of 'unauthorized software', must be anticipated up front and solutions to these issues written into the policy. As soon as senior staff detect they are being impeded by the policy then they will start to ignore it. This will therefore send out the wrong message to everyone else working with these staff.

12.5 Ownership

Although the security policy will be applicable to everyone in the organization, there must be clearly identifiable owners of the policy, and of the policy document, so that there is a means of accountability should any clarification be needed. The owner of the policy should be the head of the information systems, or similar, who may be a board member or report directly to the board. This provides the necessary gravitas for the policy to be accepted and adhered to. There should also be a single member of the information systems team, accountable to the head of information systems, who owns the actual policy document and is responsible for document maintenance and issuing new releases.

In practice, particularly in larger organizations, the document owner is unlikely to have complete responsibility for the document preparation and content. More than likely, several individuals will co-author the document and will provide the necessary clarity and exactness that the document warrants. The document, when released, should then be signed and authorized by the board, preferably by the managing director.

Each individual who is involved in the policy documentation must have the necessary authority to act in the capacity assigned to them. Key parts of the policy document will have owners assigned to them. These owners should be clearly stated so that there is a clear, single point of contact for any discussion policy. This need not be the same person or role mentioned above as being responsible for the implementation of the policy.

At the risk of repetition, paramount to the document's success is the involvement of the board, because that provides the authority required. Information systems are a business system and the policy should be treated as a business document and not just another memo from IT.

12.6 Format

The format of the security policy document should be dictated by the needs of your organization. Broadly speaking, there are two different formats that can be adopted, single document format or multiple document format.

12.6.1 The single document format

A single document can be the most accessible format in that the document is self-contained and therefore by definition completely inclusive. This is the document format that most organizations should strive for. The problem with a single document format is that the breadth and coverage required by a larger organization might make the document too large for easy consumption and comprehension. In this instance multiple documents may be required.

12.6.2 The multiple document format

This document format is most suited for larger organizations that have a commensurate breadth and depth to their policy that might be too much for a single document. The first volume should be a set of mandatory procedures that provide a brief digest of the security policy with little or no added explanation. A second, and larger, volume that contains guidance and insight can be written in support of the digest. The larger volume can be used as a background source of information to complement the mandatory procedures. Both documents should be given the same document number and labelled part A and B or main part and appendix.

Another way could be to have a multiple document format where there could be a single mandatory document, but accompanied by a multiple document set that encompasses guidance for using email, the World Wide Web, data backup, and an acceptable use policy. Each of these documents should have a distinct document number. In this way individuals should be able to grasp the salient points of each facet of security without being dwarfed by the complexity and size of a single document. Remember, if the policy document is not read, then the policy will not be adhered to and will therefore be useless.

12.6.3 Paper or electronic format?

The security policy document should be held in the same document format as the rest of the business systems documentation. Whether or not policies should be updated regularly is a moot point for those interested in procedures. For an area of activity like information systems, where technology changes frequently, the chances are that the security policy document will need to be updated fairly frequently, particularly as legal issues concerning encryption and the monitoring of business email continue to evolve. Electronic formats are easier to monitor and update, often proving to be more dynamic than their paper counterparts, and for this reason you may consider distributing your policy document in electronic format.

An additional benefit of using electronic formatted documents is that they can be deployed on everyone's desktop by using the intranet. By deploying the policy at the desktop, perhaps by a hyperlink or icon, the policy document is accessible by all. Browsing a policy statement by using the word search capability of a word processor is far easier than walking down the corridor and leafing through a paper copy. Problems of control are easily dealt with by using a macro to write an appropriate banner within the document header or footer.

12.7 Benefits

At this stage, the benefits of the security policy should be clearly understood. You are probably convinced of the need to have a security policy, but you still have to convince your board in order to get the backing that you need. The benefits of policy from an IT point of view are all well and good, but to be accepted by the board these benefits must all translate into a reduction in overheads and risk. These are the real benefits that you need to quote to the board in order to get support for the security policy. After all, what senior manager would not relish the opportunity to cut their overheads by a substantial amount? The benefits of drafting and implementing a security policy can therefore be quoted as follows:

- A more secure network infrastructure.
- A more educated workforce.

- More transparency of the network's administration within the organization.
- Fewer incidences of security breaches.
- Less downtime and denial of service.
- Less impact of breaches.
- A more fluid working environment.
- A consequential reduction of lost time and therefore reduction in overheads.

Some of the often-quoted statistics, as reported in Chapter 1, are provided again here for your reference:

- Most organizations, 69 per cent, hold information on their network that is classed as sensitive or critical.
- Between 1998 and 2000, 60 per cent of all organizations reported a security breach.
- These breaches cost anywhere from £20 000 to in excess of £100 000 per breach.
- Security breaches are on the increase.

12.8 Content

The content of the security policy will be largely dictated by:

- The size of your organization.
- The nature of your business.
- The various risks that show up during the risk analysis that you should carry out prior to the drafting of the policy.

To a greater or lesser degree the security policy should include the following subject areas. Example policy statements have been included in some areas, to start you thinking about how these statements can be written. Use and adapt these if you wish, but be aware that you will most likely require greater detail in some areas. Also note that in some cases these statements might be entirely inappropriate for your organization! Only you know what is appropriate and what is not.

12.8.1 Introduction

The opening section of the policy should start by describing the importance of the networked information systems to the organization, the value of the data held on the information systems, and the limited time period during which your organization could operate without access to that data. This enables you then to assert the need to ensure that the information systems are used within a defined set of policy rules and obligations that are incumbent on employees and the organization alike.

Applicability

Next state in definitive terms the applicability of the security policy to the organization. State clearly that the policy applies to everyone that uses the organization's networked information systems, regardless of position, status or role within the organization. If adherence to the policy is part of the terms and conditions of employment, then say so, and lay down the consequences of failure to comply. If the policy is part of any other procedural framework, such as ISO 9000, then say so.

12.8.2 Management framework

The management framework section of the policy should describe the roles and responsibilities of those who are involved in planning, implementing, maintaining and enforcing the security policy.

Main board

A representative from the main board should be indicated in order to give the policy the formal support necessary for widespread acceptance.

Stakeholders

Then the management framework will include an indication of the relationship between other policy stakeholders, such as the helpdesk, the system administrators, the support team, the Web master and Web development team, and the users.

Security administrator

A security manager or administrator should be named, as should the document owner, and the team responsible for writing and collating the document.

Reporting

There should be a clear indication of the reporting and escalation structure, showing first points of contact, with contact details, that users should contact if certain events occur, such as virus infection or loss of data files. The best way of representing this information might be on an organization chart, with names and roles, indicated clearly. If this organization chart were placed on the organization's intranet, then hyperlinks could lead to more information about each role on the chart.

12.8.3 Legal framework for information systems

An introduction to the legal framework for information systems use should come early on in the security policy in order to lay the foundations for later directives on acceptable use, particularly with regard to email, the Web, and data processing. Referring to relevant parliamentary Acts at various parts of the policy gives the acceptable use directives rather more gravitas; without any legal grounding, acceptable use directives are in danger of making the organization appear to be draconian for the sake of things, or, worse still, to appear arbitrary. Notable parliamentary Acts include the following, but there may be others that you might wish to include:

- Defamation Act 1996.
- Trade Description Act 1968.
- Consumer Protection Act 1987.
- Trade Marks Act 1994.
- Obscene Publications Act 1959.
- Copyright, Designs and Patents Act 1988.
- Data Protection Act 1998.
- Computer Misuse Act 1990.
- Electronics Communications Act 2000.
- Regulation of Investigatory Powers Act 2000.

Legal precedents

Alert employees to the fact that there have been several high profile cases recently that have resulted in the successful prosecution of individuals or organizations arising out of the misuse of networked information systems. Give instances of various cases that give clear precedent to the way individuals or organizations have been found to have acted unlawfully.

The company, directors, and employees are bound to use networked information systems, including computer workstations, in accordance with the laws of Great Britain and Northern Ireland, including but not restricted to the Data Protection Act 1998, Libel and the Defamation Act 1996, and Computer Misuse Act 1990.

In recent years, there have been many instances of misuse, deliberate or otherwise, which have been found to be in breach of various Acts, particularly with regard to the use of company email. Be aware that misuse of company networked information systems may lead to successful prosecution of the company, directors, or employees.

Right to privacy in the workplace

What degree of privacy can employees expect when using their computers? Will you be:

- Scanning emails in transit to and from your organization using content scanning software?
- Monitoring a user's email?
- Will you be storing email that has been sent or received, in addition to storage carried out by users?
- Permitting or prohibiting users to encrypt their email or personal files?
- Conducting audits of user's file storage space?
- Checking log files to review activity on the web?

If you plan to do any of these, then this should be stated in the legal section of the policy, with reference to any Acts of Parliament or legal guidance that permit your organization to do so. This should help to manage users' expectations of privacy.

Measures in place to ensure compliance with the company's legal obligations include email content scanning, and the periodic audit and review of network activity and file storage. The company reserves the right, in exceptional circumstances, to read email sent to and from company systems, while not abusing any duty to individual's privacy.

Let's not forget the right to privacy that our customers have.

The use of personal data gathered from customers shall be regulated by directives from the designated company data controller, and shall be in accordance with the Data Protection Act 1998.

12.8.4 Inventory

The security policy should contain a statement about the protection and security of hardware and software assets.

Asset tagging

The inventory you took earlier may have resulted in the application of asset tags onto pieces of equipment, in order that each piece of hardware can be identified against the inventory records. Employees should be alerted to the need to ensure that these tags are not removed, and warned if anti-theft tags are being used.

All hardware and software shall be asset tagged for identification and reference against inventory records. These tags can aid the recovery of equipment if stolen and must not be removed.

Removal or relocation of assets

Procedures for the removal or relocation of assets should be documented, as should procedures for the writing-off or disposal of assets. This is another area in which the prospect of uncontrolled software should be addressed.

An inventory of network assets is taken each year, with conformance checks each month, in accordance with company guidelines for audit. In order that the location of assets can be monitored, the removal of assets normally situated within the company premises, such as computers or printers, shall be in accordance with company procedure 1234A.

12.8.5 Physical security

Physical security is in many instances not given the attention warranted. This is unfortunate, as lax physical security procedures can bring to nothing all of the other security measures you put in place, and implementing physical security measures is relatively simple. Take into consideration the following areas within your security policy, and do not neglect to pay attention to other key hardware, such as printers, and networking equipment.

Access controls that apply to your premises

You should identify what access controls are used within your organization in order that personnel, whether employees or otherwise, can enter the premises in general, and also the secure computing area in particular. Do personnel require escorting? Must visitors wear identification badges? Must staff use a different entrance to visitors? Whatever measures are in place should be described clearly.

All visiting personnel shall sign in at reception and shall be escorted within the company premises by their sponsor.

All personnel entering company premises shall wear company identification badges or visitor badges obtained from the visitors' reception following signing in by the visitor's sponsor. Visitors shall not be permitted to enter into restricted areas.

Requirements for the secure housing of the network servers and other equipment

Network servers need to be afforded enough physical protection so that they are not at risk of interference by any unauthorized party. This usually means putting the server within a secure room or area with access controls. The same protection should be provided to any host servers that are connected to the Internet, and to other network equipment. You will probably wish to specify within the policy the mandatory protection to be provided, together with minimum requirements for air conditioning, and UPS facilities.

Company servers shall be situated in a secure area. Access to the secure area by designated network administrators or system administrators shall be controlled by keypad locks. The secure area shall contain protection measures adequate to ensure the continued and uninterrupted operation of hardware stored within, including air conditioning and an uninterruptible power supply.

Specification for cabling

When cabling is routed throughout workspaces, the original routing is usually well installed, perhaps as part of the original building work. Older buildings, or those organizations that have undertaken several office moves, might have cabling that is more ad hoc. If you have certain minimum requirements for cabling, such as type of cable, method of installation, protection against fire, then list them in the policy.

All cabling shall be routed through installed trunking and shall be deployed by network administrators or technicians only.

Power supply cables shall be plugged into installed wall or floor sockets only, no extension leads or socket doublers shall be used.

Data storage and backup

Users should be encouraged or mandated to store data on the server facilities in order that data is regularly backed up. This should be specified in the policy. Some organizations use removable media, and then store media containing sensitive data in a locking cabinet. If you use removable hard disks for this purpose, or other media, then specify what the storage procedures are.

Data storage facilities are provided for all users and administrators within the fileserver. In order that users' data is regularly backed up, users shall not store data on their local computer workstation's hard disk.

Users equipped with removable hard disks for the storage of sensitive data shall store the hard drive within a lockable cabinet during their absence from the premises.

Anti-theft measures

Asset tagging of equipment might be discussed again in this section, as should any additional security measures deployed such as the use of steel cables that can be used to secure computers or other equipment to the desk or racking.

In order to reduce the likelihood of equipment theft, all hardware and software is asset tagged with tamper-proof labels. In addition, computer monitors and base units are marked with the company name and postcode visible to the naked eye.

Equipment kept in public areas shall be fixed securely to the desk or work surface on which the equipment is situated using approved security fixings.

Portable equipment

Finally, you should include policy for the safe and secure use of portable equipment such as notebook computers. The importance of asset tagging and cables should be underlined again, but you should also include guidance for preventing the theft of equipment when on the move. Remind employees to store notebook computers out of site, and that vendor branded carry bags are not the most discrete carry bags to use.

Notebook computers are easily stolen. When travelling by car, store the notebook computer out of site in the car boot. Carry the notebook in an anonymous carry case in order not to advertise the notebook to potential thieves.

Use the security cable provided to secure the notebook while working away from your home or office if you have to leave the notebook in an unfamiliar environment.

Do not store sensitive material on the notebook hard disk or on floppy disks.

Notebook hard disks shall be encrypted using approved encryption software installed by the system administrator or technicians only. The password used within the encryption shall be different to that used within your user account.

12.8.6 Maintenance and other procedures

The security policy should contain procedures and guidance about the correct maintenance of hardware and software. Notes on the procedure for procurement and upgrade of hardware and software should be included together with the details of the individuals who are responsible for implementing the upgrades.

Desktop configuration

If the operating system has been configured so that new software cannot be installed by the user then that policy should be stated.

Desktop computers are provided with a standard range of office applications, presented in a uniform desktop workspace. Additional software applications will not normally be required. In the event that users require a specific application which is not part of the standard range, their system administrator should be contacted in the first instance.

All desktop computers are configured so that removable drives can be accessed by administrative account users only.

Escalation

There should be a designated escalation route for users to follow in the case of help being required. Certain events that might warrant special attention are discussed in a later section. Basic support procedures should be documented here as well, including the role of the helpdesk and points of contact.

In the event of their desktop computer, or other equipment being used, failing during operation, users should contact the system support representative attached to their office area. Contact names and numbers for representatives are available on the company intranet. In the event of there not being immediate resolution, the problem will be raised with the helpdesk who will resolve the problem or call out a system technician or administrator.

Event reporting

The security policy should contain procedures and guidance about the management of various events such as:

- Virus infection
  If you suspect that a virus, Trojan, or similar, has entered your desktop computer, log out and turn your computer off. Call the helpdesk immediately. Be ready to describe the incident and to give the location where your workstation is situated.
- Discovery of a breach in security
  No matter how trivial they may seem, security breaches have the potential to escalate and cause serious loss or damage to the company. If you suspect a breach has occurred, call the helpdesk immediately. Be ready to describe the incident
- Data restoration
  Backup copies of data stored on network drives are made at daily intervals by the system administrative staff. In the event of data found to be missing from your user area, contact the helpdesk immediately in order that data can be restored. Be ready to provide your account name and the names or details of missing files. Restoration will not be instantaneous.

Account management

Establish a lifecycle for account management, from account creation to account deletion, and the allocation of account privilege. Ensure that personnel have input into the lifecycle. How are file access permissions set?

User accounts are created following submission of form 123b to the helpdesk, by the recruiting officer from within personnel, to be submitted following the issue of joining instructions to a new member of staff.

On the termination of contract of employment, user accounts are deleted following submission of form 123c to the helpdesk. This form should be completed by the personnel officer or manager conducting the exit interview.

Instigation of the business continuity processes

In the event of a disaster that could impact upon the continued operation of the organization, you will need to be quick to instigate the procedures for ensuring business continuity. Any delay could impede the subsequent migration to alternate premises, or jeopardize the smooth handover of operations. The policy must state who has the authority to instigate the continuity process, and how that process is actioned.

In the event of a fire, act of God, or some other disaster that makes continued use of the networked information systems or the premises unlikely, the procedure for business continuity shall be instigated. Instigation of the procedure may be carried out by any director or senior manager, who shall inform the helpdesk of their intention. The helpdesk shall then initiate the business continuity procedure as documented in section 12 of the company network security policy.

Police involvement

What is the procedure for calling in the police in the event of unauthorized access or some other legal breach? What is the policy on prosecution of offenders? Most importantly, will your local police even appreciate the significance of a set of circumstances that might constitute a crime and will they know how to respond?

Deliberate or unauthorized misuse of the networked information systems, contrary to the policy and guidance contained herein, may constitute a criminal act. In such cases, following a review of the circumstances by a company director or senior manager, police involvement may be sought.

12.8.7 Operating system configuration

The security policy should contain procedures and guidance concerning the configuration of the operating systems in widespread use throughout the organization. Avoid writing a complete technical description, though, as this might be of help to those who may wish to gain unauthorized access. If a specific procedure is followed when computers are configured, then this should be documented elsewhere, and referred to at this stage in passing only. Some of the items to cover are as follows.

Baseline installation

Baseline operating system configuration, including policy on vendor, minimum specification product, and major and minor release of the operating system with minimum patch level.

Desktop computers shall be Pentium II or greater, have 124 MB RAM or greater, and be installed with Microsoft Windows NT 4 with Service Pack 6a.

Design studio computers shall be installed with Apple OS X.

Specific installation options used, such as the basic desktop layout, or deviations from standard out-of-the-box installation.

The standard installation shall include DHCP networking enabled.

Notebook computers shall be installed with hardware profiles so that network access by modem or by PCMCIA card network device can be selected by the user at bootup.

Specific add-ons used (Microsoft Windows NT Policy Editor, Microsoft add-on strong password filter).

The standard installation of Windows NT 4 shall include the Microsoft C2 compliance patch and the strong password dll filter.

Specific criteria that the installed operating system must fulfil, in order that operational security is maintained, should be stated.

All operating systems and firewalls used within the organization shall be certified to E3 level against the ITSEC evaluation criteria.

Patches and service packs

How are upgrades and patches going to be applied, and who will do this?

Operating system service packs and patches shall be installed by the system administrator or technician, following an appraisal of the derived benefits of the pack or patch, and normally within two weeks of release for service packs and within one day of patch release.

Or

All software updates are installed as and when available. Installation is automated, users will be required to follow any reboot instructions required following installation. Errors that occur during installation should be treated as a problem required to be escalated to the helpdesk.

12.8.8 Network services

This section of the policy should contain an itemized list of the network services that are permitted for use within the organization's network. The role of a firewall in controlling or monitoring this policy should be made clear to users and administrators alike so that there is no gap between policy and practice.

Network access controls

Are you going to ban modems?

Secure and protected access to the Internet is provided through the company network gateway. In order that security measures are not inadvertently bypassed, modems shall not be used on desktop workstations, or on laptop computers while connected to the network.

Do you use a firewall?

To protect the company networked information systems from unauthorized access and other threats, distributed firewalls are in place between the company network and the Internet, which act as choke points and filters for all network traffic to and from the network. Firewalls are used within the company network in order to control the flow of network traffic between geographically remote sections.

The default policy

Is the default policy a deny all or permit all?

The World Wide Web and email can be accessed from the Internet through the organization's firewall. All other services are unable to pass through the firewall.

In order to preserve network capacity, users should avoid using streaming media or multimedia files from the Internet.

12.8.9 Passwords

The security policy should contain procedures and guidance about the correct use of passwords. This should include specification of the way in which passwords are enforced within the operating system, so users are aware of any restrictions, without having to find out the hard way. Guidance should be included concerning minimum password length, and relative strength of the password with the inclusion of mixed alphanumeric characters. Users should be warned of the dangers of disclosing their passwords to third parties, and alerted to the fact that a system administrator would be unlikely to ever require the password of a user account. Why not start by alerting the user to the following points?

All users are reminded of the following rules for setting passwords:

The password shall be distinct from the account name and any derivative thereof.

The password shall be distinct from a dictionary word from any language.

Numerical prefixes or suffixes shall not be used with passwords that do not comply with the above clauses.

The password shall contain upper and lower case characters.

The password should contain a mix of numerical and alphabet characters, perhaps with control characters in order to protect accounts that can access sensitive information.

Passwords shall be changed at intervals of not greater than six weeks.

In addition, for administrators to take note of:

Administrative passwords shall be changed whenever staff with administrative accounts depart the organization.

12.8.10 Software controls

Software controls are on occasions not given the attention they deserve. Not only can uncontrolled software lead to problems with unlicensed use, but software that has not been properly tested and then released and installed in a controlled manner can lead to an unstable workstation, prone to crashing. These are security risks that can be addressed within the security policy.

Where shall software be installed? Under what conditions can software be released from storage?

Software CDs are stored within a lockable cabinet, within the helpdesk bureau, and may be used by helpdesk personal or released to network and system administrators only. Network and system administrators may keep backup copies of installation media for everyday use.

Can users install software themselves?

Approved software only shall be installed on computer workstations. Installation shall only be carried out by system technicians or administrators. Requests for software required to be approved should be submitted on form XYZ, available on the intranet.

Can users copy software?

In order to satisfy licensing arrangements, copies of software disks may not be made, except for use by IT staff during routine installation and maintenance.

Can users install software on their home computers?

Corporate software may be used on all computers owned by the company. Corporate software may not be installed on any other computer.

What is the procedure for installing software?

Should software be required on a computer workstation, a request for installation should be made to the helpdesk in the first instance. Requests shall be responded to within one day, subject to licensing availability.

Can users install and use personal software that they own?

Software to be used on the company workstations shall be provided by the company, unauthorized or personal software may not be used.

12.8.11 Acceptable use

The security policy should contain procedures and guidance for acceptable use of the system. This is the section of the policy that if not written carefully can make the policy appear unnecessarily draconian. So, perhaps refer again to the legal framework, with special reference to libel, data protection, and indecency.

Users should be reminded that computers and network facilities within the organization are business tools to be used for business related activities only. You should also include any constraints you may wish to make, after careful consideration of the business case, to the use of accounts. This should include information about the following aspects.

Permitted hours of use

When will you permit users to log on and utilize their desktop workstation accounts? Will you permit working beyond normal working hours? Will you permit use at any time of the day or night?

User accounts shall be available for use between 07:00 hours and 21:00 hours. Access to user accounts outside of these times may be arranged by calling the helpdesk.

Portability of accounts between workstations or users

The resources attributed to a user account, such as data files, access to applications, and access to printers and other hardware, are normally able to be accessed from any workstation in an office, not just the workstation that a user might normally call 'their computer'. Similarly, user accounts can be accessed by any person who has the account name and password. Unless you are a strong advocate of hot desking and have the necessary supporting infrastructure in place, you might wish to insert clauses in your policy that ensure that user accounts are tied to specific workstations. You should certainly insert clauses that caution strongly against user accounts being shared!

User account names and associated passwords shall not be divulged to any third party. Other users, or administrators, have no requirement to know your account name and password, and you should not divulge your password details.

Your user account will normally only be able to be accessed from your designated workstation. Should you require access to your account from another workstation, this can be arranged by calling the helpdesk.

Limitations on disk space

Disk space is a valuable commodity. Many organizations find that their server storage space can, unchecked, fill to near capacity, which poses a threat to the stability of the file server. For this reason some organizations choose to allocate disk quotas so that users have a limit to the amount of storage space they can use. The limit is often set so that there is a soft boundary.

Users are allocated a disk storage quota of 250 MB. Data in excess of this limit will be stored for seven days, after which archiving of the oldest files will take place automatically. Restoration of archived files shall be provided by contacting the system administrator.

Restrictions on personal use

For many organizations, the policy is clear: computers are there for business use only. However, this is both unduly draconian and unrealistic. You need to decide whether or not personal use will pose a security threat to your secure network. So, although you may not permit use of personal software, or the personal use of email, you might permit the use of office productivity applications for personal use or the use of the World Wide Web, subject to restrictions. Clearly, running a business using the organization's facilities is not on, but writing an essay for submission as part of an Open University course might well be an activity that should be encouraged.

Personal use of the organization's network information systems is permitted for private, non-profit making activities, subject to compliance with other pertinent clauses herein.

Or

The network information systems are for use in pursuance of the organization's activities only.

Password controlled screensaver

A workstation left unattended, with the account open, is dangerous. Anyone else can make use of that account, to steal information or just to cause annoyance. For this reason, users should be encouraged to log out of their computers whenever they are absent from their desks for some period of time. The time period will be dependent on their working environment.

Screensavers should be password protected and set to become active following three minutes of inactivity. Lock your workstation when you

are absent from your desk for any reason. Log off when you anticipate being absent from your desk for more than 30 minutes.

Data classification

What security are you applying to the actual data that you are storing on your networks? Do you classify information? If so you will need to explain the significance of the classifications to users, and whether certain information can be sent externally to the organization or taken offsite.

Users' data files and documents shall be protective marked if they contain sensitive information, and stored so that access is permitted only to other personnel that are authorized to view such data. Protectively marked data or files shall not normally be sent outside the organization via email, or any other means. Advice and guidance on the storage and handling of classified data can be obtained from the helpdesk in the first instance.

12.8.12 Email

Secure use of email is a principle area of network use that should be carefully regulated within the secure network environment. The legal standing of email needs to be defined clearly, in order that personnel are clear about the implications of sending email without due care. Remind users of the following aspects.

Email is an insecure form of communication

Employees need to be aware that email is not a private means of communication in the same way that a written letter is. Perhaps a better analogy is to liken an email to a fax. Like a facsimile, you never really know who will read the email message. For these reasons, emails should not contain material or discussion that is classified or sensitive, unless you are going to employ encryption.

Email is an insecure form of communication and should be used for communications that are deemed to be public domain. Private, sensitive, or classified information should be sent by an alternative means of communication.

Email is a corporate communication

The organization from where an email message originates can usually be readily identified. Often the email domain name in the address will have been well marketed in association with the website address, and so will be readily associated with the organization. For this reason, you may conclude that email shall be used for communications on behalf of the organization only. If you are not going to ban personal use, then you might instead choose to discourage the forwarding of chain letters, or similar, sent by email.

Email shall be used in pursuance of the organization's business aims only. Use of email for personal communication is prohibited.

Or

Email messages that may be deemed to be spam, chain mail, junk mail, lewd or otherwise inappropriate material shall not be sent, forwarded, or otherwise distributed using the company email system. Receipt of such email, while not always avoidable, should nevertheless be discouraged by users.

Composition

Email is a rapid form of communication. You might remind employees that email should be read and spell checked prior to sending, and that credibility can be given to the email message by the use of a more formal style of writing.

Any email you send is sent on behalf of the company. Therefore, email shall be written in the same style as a business letter. As in all company communications, colloquialisms and casual turns of phrases should be used sparingly. Use a spell checker before you send your message.

Legality

Email has the same legal standing, within many jurisdictions, as other forms of written communication. This has certainly been demonstrated in the UK and in the US by case law. Therefore, employees should be obliged to take great care when sending email. Communication by email should be regarded in the same way as a letter sent on company headed paper.

Email messages can be used in evidence within courts of law and other tribunals. Care should be taken to ensure that your email contains the message you wish to convey, and that the email does not expose the organization to liability through misrepresentation, defamation, or similar.

Use of email attachments

Attachments have the potential to cause many security problems. They consume resources, have the potential to introduce viruses, and in some cases might contain inappropriate content. For this reason you should consider whether or not to introduce the following guidance.

Only company documents should be attached to emails.

This is a one way of limiting the use of attachments, and therefore the potential for harm from inappropriate content, or other threats. Are you going to permit or deny the use of JavaScript, Java, VBScript and ActiveX within email attachments? You should give careful consideration to each of these active content types, and consider backing up any policy directive with content control measures.

Are you going to encourage attachments to be compressed using pkzip or tar utilities? This might be one way of being more liberal, but consuming fewer resources.

Attachments shall be used to send documentation or data in pursuance of the organization's business aims. For the benefit of the recipient as well as the company, users are encouraged to use file compression tools, such as pkzip or similar to reduce the attachment size. Attachments that contain VBScript or ActiveX are not able to be sent.

Disclaimers

What disclaimers, if any, should be used? The use of disclaimers seems to be universal among organizations, a practice that seems to have originated from the American legal profession where client/attorney confidentiality is protected fiercely. But, in the UK, check first with your legal department or legal counsel whether these have any legal standing within the context in which you use email.

Be under no illusion, a disclaimer will not provide anything like the legal immunity which some would expect. If you decide to use any form of disclaimer, or some other form of footer, then you will need to define the wording to be used within your policy. Users should be informed of the need to configure their email client application to attach the message to their email.

All emails should contain the company standard disclaimer, which shall be worded as follows: 'This email is a communication on behalf of company XYZ, registered business 123456. Notification of this email being sent in error would be gratefully received.'

Your email application is configured to include the disclaimer within all email messages sent. If you suspect this is not the case, please inform the helpdesk.

12.8.13 World Wide Web

Many of the issues that affect the use of email will also be pertinent to the use of the Web. The security policy should include a statement about the use of the Web to view inappropriate imagery or literature. Any restrictive policy which is actioned at the firewall should be specified so that users are aware of any restriction up front. The following points should be considered for inclusion:

Limitations of use

Shall you be prohibiting users from visiting certain websites? Consider the web-based email providers such as hotmail, adult websites, or perhaps online share broking sites. How will you enforce this prohibition? What about personal use of the Web?

Although personal use of the World Wide Web is permitted, users should take reasonable care to ensure that their use is not contrary to other clauses contained herein, in addition to compliance with legal directives.

Certain types of website are unable to be accessed through the organization's Internet gateway. These include web-based email sites, some sites that involve financial transactions, and sites that contain content inappropriate to the workplace.

Inappropriate content

You should pay particular attention to this aspect of the Web, if for no other reason than the recent high profile incidents that have led to widespread dismissal of employees. There should be no possibility of a de-facto toleration of inappropriate content being distributed arising out of a failure to document any policy that is in place.

Users shall take all steps possible to ensure that indecent or obscene material is not knowingly downloaded.

Downloading software

In order to minimize the threat from virus infection, and also to minimize the potential for uncontrolled software, you should insert clauses that prevent the ad hoc downloading and installation of software from the Web. You may wish to enforce this with technical solutions, while at the same time providing support for those who wish to evaluate software or download release updates for specialist applications not in general use.

Software executable files are normally unable to be downloaded from the Web. Users wishing to download software in pursuance of their responsibilities within the organization should contact the helpdesk for further assistance.

Active content

Are you going to permit or deny the use of JavaScript, Java, VBScript and ActiveX within the World Wide Web? Whatever your policy is, you need to manage user expectations.

Active content poses a significant threat to security. For this reason VBScript and ActiveX controls that reside within Web pages are unable to be downloaded to the organization's network. These types of content should be disabled within the Web browser. Similar preventative measures apply to all incoming email.

Multimedia and streaming media

Are you going to permit the downloading of certain types of file, such as mp3, streaming media, mpegs or avi files? If not, then you will need to prevent their downloading through the firewall, although be aware that some media applications can stream data through port 80, the port designated for http. Make sure you are discouraging the use of such applications for technical issues, such as capacity, and that you are not addressing productivity issues within your security policy.

Multimedia data can consume network resources, and for this reason is not normally permitted to be downloaded. This includes mpeg, avi, mp3, real audio files and similar.

12.8.14 Business continuity

Data restoration and disaster recovery plans should be summarized in this section, although some organizations will itemize their full procedures in a separate document. Attention should be paid to the safe transit, storage and retrieval of the backed-up data so that both the availability and security of the data can be assured.

Data backup media shall be stored within a lockable cabinet, within a secure server area. By way of mitigation in the event of the backup media being destroyed when required, a copy of the backup media shall be maintained in secure premises no more than half an hours transit to company premises and to any alternative premises used in the event of evacuation.

Appropriate disaster recovery plans need to be established

and rehearsed in order that organizations can continue to operate in such events. There must be clear and unambiguous criteria laid down formally, which give an unequivocal go ahead to action the plan. Moreover, the authority to action the plan must be ascertained. The ability to invoke the plan must be delegated to key figures throughout the organization.

In the event that the capacity of the organization to continue operation is likely to be impossible, through act of God, disaster, building or network information system failure, the procedure for business continuity shall be invoked by a company director, or senior manager that has the verbal authorization of a company director.

All staff need to know where to congregate, and who to report to in the new location. Everyone needs to know their role in the continuation process, and the escalation chain when certain events occur.

Invocation of business continuity plans shall be announced on the company PA system, or by similar announcement, which must be acted on immediately. On hearing the announcement, all personnel shall perform duties, and report problems, according to procedures stated within document XYZ.

12.8.15 Technical solutions employed to re-enforce the policy

The security policy should contain procedures and guidance about the measures used to secure the system, in general terms only. If a firewall is used, there is no need to specify which particular application is used but the policy implemented in the firewall should be specified.

The organization's networked information systems are connected to the Internet in order to facilitate communication with clients, partners, and suppliers. This connection is moderated and controlled by a firewall, which performs the following functions:

- *Limits external access to the organization's network.*
- *Prevents harmful or damaging content from passing into the network.*
- *Provides anonymity to users.*

Because the firewall filters all traffic, according to the policy contained herein, a slight degradation in network speed may be perceptible at times.

In the case of encryption being used, what applications should be used? How are keys issued? How is the encryption software requested, installed, and distributed?

Some users have the facility provided for the encryption of files and data. This may be because a notebook computer is being used, or because files or data contain particularly sensitive information. If you feel that you require encryption, you should contact the helpdesk in the first instance.

Encryption keys are issued by a designated key controller. Encryption software other than that provided by the organization shall not be used in any circumstances.

Who is responsible for installing virus protection software?

Virus protection software shall be installed on each workstation or server computer, and shall be installed at the interface between the organization's network and the Internet. Virus protection software shall be administered by the system administrator. If you suspect you have no virus protection software installed, please notify the helpdesk.

12.9 Security policy: the project overview

The drafting and launch of the security policy should be treated as a project, with a definite requirement, i.e. a formal security policy, and a definite timescale to be determined in the preliminary planning process. As a rule of thumb, most organizations could draft and implement a security policy within six months. Several tasks can be identified in the project. These are itemized below. Prior to launching your plan, though, you need to get the board on your side. You know your organization best, but most busy executives would be happy to read a project proposal that contains the following:

- The convincing case for a security policy: this should include some well-researched information about the overheads incurred due to security breaches and the threats and risks that are pertinent to your organization. If you can provide metrics derived from your own user community, these will be more convincing than generic statistics which have the shock value but perhaps not the applicability. The case should also include quantitative estimates of the overhead savings that can be made.
- An outline project plan: this needs to contain the projected time frame that conforms to their expectation of how long a project like this would take for completion, and also a work breakdown structure or a Gantt chart. The key players should be identified and their availability should be confirmed beforehand.
- A budget: this should include the projected costs arising from

the taskings in the Gantt chart and should also include the cost of any new software, hardware or additional expertise that needs to be introduced. This budget should conform to the expectations for how much a project of this nature should cost. The budget should be compared to the potential overhead savings to make a compelling case.

- The ability for the key decision maker to 'turn key' and start the project, there and then, without any further consultation required on your part.

12.10 Implementation

When the draft policy has been reviewed and the final document put together, the time will come for the security policy to be issued. Accompanying the security policy should be a formal launch. This could take the form of a launch party, or a series of launch seminars that will raise the awareness of the security policy in most users' minds. This launch should include some background awareness of the need for a security policy as well as a discussion of the policy document. Following the launch activity, the policy document must be maintained as part of the organization's procedure set.

12.11 Review

- The security policy places network security issues in a context whereby they can be readily understood, appreciated, and followed by the entire user community.
- The policy should define the problem domain, define responsibility, educate, and therefore reduce the incidence of security breaches.
- The security policy should apply to everyone in the organization, without exception.
- Ownership of the policy should be designated to individuals who are responsible for maintaining or writing the document.
- The format of the document will vary according to the needs of your organization. A single document may suffice, but many choose to have a high-level security policy that refers to other specific documents, for instance a specific document concerning disaster recovery.
- Whatever the format, the document should be distributed in electronic and printed formats.
- The production of the policy should be managed as a project, with activities, timescales, and a deliverable, that has the backing of the board of directors.

- The security policy should be implemented with a launch party or event, so that the entire organization knows that a security policy exists.

Index

For Product Safety Concerns and Information please contact our EU representative GPSR@taylorandfrancis.com Taylor & Francis Verlag GmbH, Kaufingerstraße 24, 80331 München, Germany

Printed and bound by CPI Group (UK) Ltd, Croydon, CR0 4YY
01/05/2025
01858340-0001